cook's library
Potatoes

cook's library
Potatoes

p

This is a Parragon Book
First published in 2003

Parragon
Queen Street House
4 Queen Street
Bath BA1 1HE, UK

ISBN: 0-75258-757-9

Printed in China

NOTE

This book uses metric and imperial measurements. Follow the same
units of measurement throughout; do not mix metric and imperial.
All spoon measurements are level: teaspoons are assumed to be 5 ml,
and tablespoons are assumed to be 15 ml. Unless otherwise stated,
milk is assumed to be full fat, eggs and individual vegetables, such as
potatoes, are medium, and pepper is freshly ground black pepper.

The times given for each recipe are an approximate guide only because
the preparation times may differ according to the techniques used by
different people and the cooking times may vary as a result of the type
of oven used. The preparation times include chilling and marinating
times, where appropriate.

Recipes using raw or very lightly cooked eggs should be
avoided by infants, the elderly, pregnant women, convalescents
and anyone suffering from an illness.

Contents

Introduction

There is a vast range of different varieties of potato – around 3,000 in all – although only about 100 of these are regularly grown. Each variety has its own distinctive shape, texture and colour, and reflects the country to which it is native, from the firm yellow flesh of the Jersey Royal new potato to the rich, warm orange of the yam from the Caribbean.

Possibly dating from as far back as 3000 BCE, the potato originated in South America, where it was known as the 'papa'. It was eaten by the Incas, fresh when it was in season and dried in winter. Its existence was not brought to the attention of the rest of the world until the 16th century, however, when Peru fell to the Spanish conquistador Francisco Pizarro. Peru was well known to be rich in minerals, and it was the mineral traders who began to introduce the potato elsewhere.

In Europe, the potato arrived via Spain, and its name gradually evolved from 'papa' to 'battata'. It became famous not only for its nutritional value, but also for its healing properties.

The Italians believed that the cooked flesh would heal a wound if rubbed into the infected area, and Pope Pius IV was sufficiently convinced of this to plant his own crop in Italy. From here, the potato moved northwards through Switzerland, France, Germany and Belgium, reaching the New World with the explorer Francis Drake, who shared his cargo of potatoes with the starving English colonists.

Sir Walter Raleigh later brought the potato to Britain. He also took it to Ireland, where the soil was perfect for growing it, and it became a dietary mainstay for the Irish peasantry, who survived for generations on very little else.

Nutritionally, potatoes are an excellent source of starch for energy and fibre. They have a higher protein value than most plant foods, are very rich in vitamin C, and also contain vitamin B-complex, as well as minerals, especially potassium. However, many of the nutrients are found in or just below the skin, so it is essential to cook them in ways that will retain their health-promoting properties.

Although potatoes were once considered to be forbidden to slimmers, they are in fact a positive aid to weight control when cooked and served with the minimum of fat. Sufferers from stomach ulcers and arthritis will also benefit from drinking raw potato juice, although their taste buds may object to the flavour!

This book is a collection of some of the most delicious and diverse potato recipes, which have been gathered from around the world. Whatever the occasion, these dishes will show you how this splendidly adaptable vegetable can be used in a multitude of ways to enhance your everyday eating.

Regional Cooking

Although the potato is known and grown throughout the world, the ways in which it is cooked and served vary enormously from country to country, and often depend on whether it is the main staple of a nation's diet.

The highest consumers are Russia, Poland and Germany, followed by Holland, Cyprus and Ireland. Elsewhere the potato may be used less than pasta, rice or bread in the daily diet.

As Spain was the first European country to discover the potato, it is appropriate that it is used in one of the most popular and well-known classic Spanish dishes, tortilla, a substantial, crispy-coated vegetable omelette-like dish of eggs and thinly sliced waxy potatoes, to which may be added peppers, tomatoes, sweetcorn – the choice is unlimited. Variations of this recipe can be found all around the Mediterranean – a Greek version, for example, involves filling the potato omelette with a melting mixture of feta cheese and spinach.

In Italy, floury potatoes are used in another classic dish – gnocchi. Here, the cooked potatoes are mashed until smooth, then mixed with flour, egg yolks and olive oil to make little dumplings, which are cooked very quickly in boiling water and served with a sauce. Herbs or cheese may be added to the basic recipe, and a delicious variation is to add spinach. A similar base can also be used to make potato noodles.

From Ireland comes Colcannon – a wonderful mixture of mashed potatoes and shredded cabbage, topped with a pool of melted butter – which is usually served with a piece of cooked bacon.

Worldwide, the potato is often used as a basis for a hearty salad. On the Mediterranean coast of France, potatoes are combined with tuna and eggs as the base for the famous Salade Niçoise. In India, they may be mixed with broccoli and mango, and topped with a spicy yogurt dressing, while in Mexico sliced potatoes are topped with tomatoes, chillies and ham and served with guacamole.

In Italy, potatoes are layered with sausage, radicchio, sun-dried tomatoes and basil and drizzled with a tomato-flavoured olive oil dressing, and in Russia the classic combination of cucumber and dill can be made more substantial by the addition of potatoes and beetroot.

The potato makes an excellent ingredient in soups, and in European cuisine, potatoes are used in a number of classic soup recipes – Vichyssoise, Pistou and Bouillabaisse, to name just a few. Different cultures also have their own variations of chowder, a filling soup based on potatoes and milk. In New England, for example, fresh clams are added, while in Scotland the chowder is flavoured with smoked haddock to make the intriguingly named Cullen Skink.

Even as an accompaniment, potatoes are served in a variety of ways. In India, for example, they are mixed with other vegetables, which readily absorb the spice flavours.

In France, layers of waxy potatoes are topped with double cream and sometimes cheese to make a rich and very filling classic dish, Potatoes Dauphinois. In Britain, they are served roasted to a crisp with the traditional Sunday lunch, and in Belgium potato chips are usually served accompanied by mayonnaise, for dipping.

Using Potatoes

The potato is without doubt one of the most versatile food items. However, not all types of potato are suitable for all purposes, and the following list gives the uses for some of the most popular varieties.

Buying and Storing

When choosing potatoes, make sure they are firm and well-shaped with a smooth, tight skin. New potatoes should be eaten as fresh as possible, but old potatoes can be stored in a cool, dark, dry place – exposure to light makes them turn green, resulting in an unpleasant flavour and a higher level of glycoalkaloids, which are naturally occurring toxins.

Craig Royal Red
This waxy, main crop potato is best for frying and boiling, or for using in salads or tortillas.

Desirée
One of the best and most versatile varieties, this pink-skinned, floury potato is good for baking, frying, boiling as well as mashing.

King Edward
A large, high-quality, creamy-white potato, this popular variety is ideal for all purposes.

Maris Piper
This medium-firm variety has creamy-white flesh, and is good for boiling and frying.

New Potatoes
These are harvested in early summer, and are best boiled and eaten warm, perhaps with chopped mint and melted butter, or cold in salads. Jersey Royals, in particular, have a superb flavour, and their appearance often heralds summer.

Pentland Crown
This creamy-white, floury potato is ideal for mashing and baking.

Yam
An orange-fleshed sweet potato, which is best mashed in cakes and soufflés, or roasted.

Preparation and Cooking

To preserve the nutritional value of potatoes, they should be baked in their skins, or scrubbed rather than peeled. If peeled potatoes are required, they should be cooked in their skins and then peeled afterwards.

Boiling

For new and old potatoes, put them in a large saucepan, pour in enough boiling water to cover, put on a lid, and boil gently until the potatoes are tender.

Steaming

To steam new and old potatoes, put them in a steamer over a saucepan of boiling water, and cook them gently until they are tender.

Mashing or Creaming

Boil the potatoes, then drain well. Add a knob of butter, season, then mash them, preferably with an electric hand-whisk, or by hand first with a potato masher and then by stirring briskly with a fork. As a variation, use garlic-infused olive oil instead of butter, add cream or crème fraîche as well as butter, or add some fresh pesto sauce.

Roasting

Simmer the potatoes in boiling water for 10 minutes. Drain, then shake them in the pan to roughen their surfaces. Put them in a roasting tray of very hot fat, and roast on the top shelf of a preheated oven, 220°C/425°F/Gas Mark 7, for 45 minutes until golden and crispy.

Baking

Scrub the potatoes, then dry them well. Prick the skins, then coat with olive oil and salt. Bake in a preheated oven, 220°C/425°F/Gas Mark 7, for 1–1½ hours.

Deep-frying

For cooking perfect chips, fritters and samosas, the temperature of the oil is all-important and a deep-fat fryer is a good investment. Par-boiled, sliced or diced potatoes can be fried or sautéed in a little oil in a heavy-based pan.

How to Use This Book

Each recipe contains a wealth of useful information, including a breakdown
of nutritional quantities, preparation and cooking times, and level of difficulty.
All of this information is explained in detail below.

A full-colour photograph
of the finished dish.

The ingredients for
each recipe are listed
in the order that they
are used.

The nutritional
information provided
for each recipe is per
serving or per portion.
Optional ingredients,
variations or serving
suggestions have not
been included in the
calculations.

The method is clearly
explained with step-by-
step instructions that
are easy to follow.

Cook's Tips provide useful
information regarding
ingredients or cooking
techniques.

17

POTATOES

These oven-baked
mushrooms are covered
with a creamy potato and
mushroom filling topped
with melted cheese.

Creamy Stuffed Mushrooms

SERVES 4

25 g/1 oz dried ceps
225 g/8 oz floury potatoes, diced
25 g/1 oz butter, melted
4 tbsp double cream
2 tbsp chopped fresh chives
8 large open-cap mushrooms
25 g/1 oz Emmenthal cheese, grated
150 ml/5 fl oz vegetable stock
salt and pepper
fresh chives, to garnish
crisp salad, to serve

1 Place the dried ceps in a small bowl. Add enough boiling water to cover and
leave to soak for 20 minutes.

2 Meanwhile, cook the potatoes in a medium saucepan of lightly salted
boiling water for 10 minutes until cooked through and tender. Drain the
potatoes well and mash until smooth.

3 Drain the ceps and chop them finely. Mix into the mashed potato.

4 Blend the butter, cream and chives together and pour the mixture into the
cep and potato mixture, mixing well. Season to taste with salt and pepper.

5 Remove the stalks from the open-cap mushrooms. Chop the stalks and stir
them into the potato mixture. Spoon the mixture into the mushrooms and
sprinkle the cheese over the top.

6 Arrange the stuffed mushrooms in a shallow ovenproof dish and pour in the
vegetable stock. Cover the dish with a lid or foil.

7 Cook in a preheated oven, 220°C/425°F/Gas Mark 7, for 20 minutes. Remove
the lid and cook for 5 minutes until golden. Transfer to a serving plate,
garnish with a few fresh chives and serve with a crisp salad.

NUTRITION
Calories 214; Sugars 1 g; Protein 5 g;
Carbohydrate 11 g; Fat 17 g; Saturates 11 g

easy
40 mins
40 mins

🔅 **COOK'S TIP**
Use fresh mushrooms instead of the dried ceps, if preferred, and stir a mixture
of chopped nuts into the mushroom stuffing mixture for extra crunch.

⭐ The number of stars represents the
difficulty of each recipe, ranging from
very easy (1 star) to challenging (4 stars).

🕐 This amount of time represents the
preparation of ingredients, including
cooling, chilling and soaking times.

🕐 This represents the cooking time.

Soups, Salads *and* Starters

Potatoes form the basis of many delicious and easy-to-prepare home-made soups, because they are the perfect thickening agent while adding a subtle flavour. With the addition of just a few ingredients, you can have a selection of soups at your fingertips. Also featured in this section are starters and salads based on potatoes. In addition to the creamy potato salads that are so popular, there are many other recipes to tempt your palate, including dishes suitable for light lunches as well as hearty main-course meals. Many are also ideal choices for barbecues and picnics.

This simple recipe uses the sweet potato with its distinctive flavour and colour, combined with a hint of orange and fresh coriander.

Sweet Potato *and* Onion Soup

SERVES 4

2 tbsp vegetable oil
900 g/2 lb sweet potatoes, diced
1 carrot, diced
2 onions, sliced
2 garlic cloves, crushed
600 ml/1 pint vegetable stock
300 ml/10 fl oz unsweetened orange juice
225 ml/8 fl oz low-fat natural yogurt
2 tbsp chopped fresh coriander
salt and pepper

to garnish
fresh coriander sprigs
strips of orange rind

1 Heat the vegetable oil in a large saucepan and add the sweet potatoes, carrot, onions and garlic. Sauté the vegetables gently for 5 minutes, stirring constantly with a wooden spoon. Do not allow to colour.

2 Pour in the vegetable stock and orange juice and bring them to the boil.

3 Reduce the heat to a simmer, cover the saucepan and cook the vegetables for 20 minutes or until the sweet potatoes and carrot are tender.

4 Transfer the mixture to a food processor or blender, in batches, and process for 1 minute until puréed. Return the purée to the rinsed-out saucepan.

5 Stir in the yogurt and coriander and season to taste with salt and pepper.

6 Ladle the soup into 4 warmed bowls and garnish with a few sprigs of fresh coriander and orange rind. Serve.

NUTRITION

Calories *320*; Sugars *26 g*; Protein *7 g*;
Carbohydrate *62 g*; Fat *7 g*; Saturates *1 g*

 easy

15 mins

30 mins

This spicy and substantial soup uses ingredients you are likely to have on hand and makes a delicious meal-in-a-bowl.

Potato *and* Chickpea Soup

1 Heat the olive oil in a large saucepan over a medium heat. Add the onion and garlic and cook for 3–4 minutes, stirring occasionally, until the onion is beginning to soften. Do not allow to colour.

2 Add the carrot, potatoes, turmeric, garam masala and curry powder to the onion and garlic and continue cooking for 1–2 minutes.

3 Add the tomatoes, water and chilli purée with a large pinch of salt. Reduce the heat, cover and simmer for 30 minutes, stirring occasionally.

4 Add the chickpeas and peas to the pan, then continue cooking for about 15 minutes or until all the vegetables are tender.

5 Taste the soup and adjust the seasoning, if necessary, adding a little more chilli, if wished. Ladle into 4 warmed soup bowls and sprinkle with coriander.

SERVES 4

1 tbsp olive oil
1 large onion, chopped finely
2–3 garlic cloves, chopped finely or crushed
1 carrot, quartered and thinly sliced
350 g/12 oz potatoes, diced
¼ tsp ground turmeric
¼ tsp garam masala
¼ tsp mild curry powder
400 g/14 oz canned chopped tomatoes
   in juice
850 ml/1½ pints water
¼ tsp chilli purée, or to taste
400 g/14 oz canned chickpeas, rinsed
   and drained
85 g/3 oz fresh or frozen peas
salt and pepper
chopped fresh coriander, to garnish

NUTRITION
Calories *40*; Sugars *1.6 g*; Protein *1.8 g*;
Carbohydrate *6.5 g*; Fat *1 g*; Saturates *0.1 g*

  moderate

5 mins

50 mins

 COOK'S TIP

If preferred, purée the soup in a blender.

A slightly hot and spicy Indian flavour is given to this soup with the use of garam masala, chilli, cumin and coriander.

Indian Potato *and* Pea Soup

SERVES 4

2 tbsp vegetable oil
225 g/8 oz floury potatoes, diced
1 large onion, chopped
2 garlic cloves, crushed
1 tsp garam masala
1 tsp ground coriander
1 tsp ground cumin
850 ml/1½ pints vegetable stock
1 red chilli, chopped
100 g/3½ oz frozen peas
4 tbsp natural yogurt
salt and pepper
chopped fresh coriander, to garnish

1 Heat the vegetable oil in a large saucepan over a low heat. Add the potatoes, onion and garlic and sauté, stirring constantly, for about 5 minutes.

2 Add the garam masala, coriander and cumin and cook, stirring constantly, for 1 minute.

3 Stir in the vegetable stock and red chilli and bring the mixture to the boil. Reduce the heat, cover the pan and simmer for about 20 minutes until the potatoes begin to break down.

4 Add the peas and cook for a further 5 minutes. Stir in the yogurt and season to taste with salt and pepper.

5 Ladle into 4 warmed soup bowls, garnish the soup with chopped fresh coriander and serve hot.

NUTRITION

Calories *160*; Sugars *8 g*; Protein *6 g*; Carbohydrate *21 g*; Fat *7 g*; Saturates *1 g*

 very easy

 5 mins

35 mins

🍳 COOK'S TIP

For slightly less heat, deseed the chilli before adding it to the soup. Always wash your hands after handling chillies because they contain volatile oils that can irritate the skin and make your eyes burn if you touch your face.

This creamy soup has a delightful pale green colouring and rich flavour from the blend of tender broccoli and blue cheese.

Broccoli *and* Potato Soup

1 Heat the olive oil in a large saucepan over a low heat. Add the potatoes and onion. Sauté the vegetables gently, stirring constantly, for 5 minutes.

2 Reserve a few broccoli florets for the garnish and add the remaining broccoli to the pan. Add the cheese and vegetable stock.

3 Bring to the boil, then reduce the heat, cover the pan and simmer for about 25 minutes until the potatoes are tender.

4 Transfer the soup to a food processor or blender, in batches, and process until the mixture is smooth. Alternatively, press the vegetables through a sieve with the back of a wooden spoon.

5 Return the purée to a clean saucepan and stir in the cream and a pinch of paprika. Season to taste with salt and pepper.

6 Blanch the reserved broccoli florets in a saucepan of boiling water for about 2 minutes, then lift them out of the pan with a slotted spoon.

7 Ladle the soup into 4 warmed soup bowls and garnish with the broccoli florets and a sprinkling of paprika. Serve immediately.

SERVES **4**

2 tbsp olive oil
450 g/1 lb potatoes, diced
1 onion, diced
225 g/8 oz broccoli florets
125 g/4½ oz blue cheese, crumbled
1 litre/1¾ pints vegetable stock
150 ml/5 fl oz double cream
pinch of paprika, plus extra to garnish
salt and pepper

NUTRITION

Calories *452*; Sugars *4 g*; Protein *14 g*; Carbohydrate *20 g*; Fat *35 g*; Saturates *19 g*

 very easy

5–10 mins

35 mins

🍳 COOK'S TIP

This soup freezes very successfully. Follow the method described here up to step 4, and freeze the soup after it has been puréed. Add the cream and paprika just before serving. Garnish and serve.

There are many varieties of dried mushrooms available on the market today; the concentrated flavour they add to a dish justifies the cost.

Potato *and* Mushroom Soup

SERVES 4

2 tbsp vegetable oil
600 g/1 lb 5 oz floury potatoes, sliced
1 onion, sliced
2 garlic cloves, crushed
1 litre/1¾ pints beef stock
25 g/1 oz dried mushrooms
2 celery sticks, sliced
2 tbsp brandy
salt and pepper

topping
40 g/1½ oz butter
2 thick slices white bread, crusts removed
50 g/1¾ oz freshly grated Parmesan cheese

to garnish
rehydrated dried mushrooms
fresh parsley sprigs

1 Heat the vegetable oil in a frying pan over a low heat. Add the potatoes, onion and garlic and sauté gently for 5 minutes, stirring constantly.

2 Add the beef stock, dried mushrooms of your choice, and the celery. Bring to the boil, then reduce the heat to a simmer, cover the saucepan and continue to cook the soup for 20 minutes until the potatoes are tender.

3 Meanwhile, melt the butter for the topping in the frying pan. Sprinkle the bread slices with the grated Parmesan cheese and fry the slices in the butter for about 1 minute on each side until crisp. Using a sharp knife, cut each slice into triangles.

4 Stir the brandy into the soup, and season to taste with salt and pepper. Ladle into 4 warmed soup bowls and top with the triangles. Garnish with a few mushrooms and sprigs of fresh parsley and serve.

NUTRITION
Calories *81*; Sugars *0.7 g*; Protein *3.8 g*;
Carbohydrate *7.6 g*; Fat *4 g*; Saturates *1.8 g*

moderate

5 mins

30 mins

COOK'S TIP

Probably the most popular dried mushroom is the cep, but any variety will add a lovely flavour to this soup. If you do not wish to use dried mushrooms, add 125 g/4½ oz sliced fresh mushrooms of your choice to the soup.

This is a really filling soup, which should be served before a light main course. It is easy to prepare and filled with flavour.

Vegetable *and* Corn Chowder

1 Heat the vegetable oil in a large saucepan over a low heat. Add the onion, pepper, garlic and potatoes and sauté, stirring frequently, for 2–3 minutes.

2 Stir in the flour and cook, stirring, for about 30 seconds. Gradually stir in the milk and vegetable stock.

3 Add the broccoli and sweetcorn. Bring the mixture to the boil, stirring constantly, then reduce the heat and simmer for about 20 minutes or until all the vegetables are tender.

4 Stir in 50 g/1¾ oz of the cheese until it melts.

5 Season to taste with salt and pepper, then spoon the chowder into a warmed soup tureen. Garnish with the remaining cheese and chopped coriander and serve.

SERVES 4

1 tbsp vegetable oil
1 red onion, diced
1 red pepper, deseeded and diced
3 garlic cloves, crushed
300 g/10½ oz potatoes, diced
2 tbsp plain flour
600 ml/1 pint milk
300 ml/10 fl oz vegetable stock
50 g/1¾ oz broccoli florets
300 g/10½ oz canned sweetcorn, drained
75 g/2¾ oz Cheddar cheese, grated
salt and pepper
1 tbsp chopped fresh coriander, to garnish

NUTRITION
Calories *378*; Sugars *20 g*; Protein *16 g*;
Carbohydrate *52 g*; Fat *13 g*; Saturates *6 g*

   COOK'S TIP

Vegetarian cheeses are made with rennets of non-animal origin.

very easy

15 mins

30 mins

It is difficult to imagine that celeriac, a coarse, knobbly and rather unattractive vegetable, can taste so sweet. It makes a delicious soup.

Celeriac, Leek *and* Potato Soup

SERVES 4

15 g/½ oz butter
1 onion, chopped
2 large leeks, halved lengthways and sliced
750 g/1 lb 10 oz celeriac, peeled and cubed
225 g/8 oz potatoes, cubed
1 carrot, quartered and thinly sliced
1.2 litres/2 pints water
⅛ tsp dried marjoram
1 bay leaf
freshly grated nutmeg
salt and pepper
celery leaves, to garnish

1 Melt the butter in a large saucepan over a medium–low heat. Add the onion and leeks and cook for 4 minutes, stirring frequently, until just softened. Do not allow to colour.

2 Add the celeriac, potatoes, carrot, water, marjoram and bay leaf, with a large pinch of salt. Bring to the boil, reduce the heat, cover and simmer for about 25 minutes until the vegetables are tender. Remove the bay leaf.

3 Leave the soup to cool slightly. Transfer to a blender or food processor and purée until smooth. (If using a food processor, strain off the cooking liquid and reserve. Purée the soup solids with enough cooking liquid to moisten them, then combine with the remaining liquid.)

4 Return the puréed soup to the saucepan and stir to blend the ingredients thoroughly. Season the soup with nutmeg, salt and pepper to taste, then simmer over a medium–low heat until reheated.

5 Ladle the soup into 4 warmed bowls, garnish with celery leaves and serve.

NUTRITION
Calories 20; Sugars 1.3 g; Protein 1.3 g;
Carbohydrate 2.7 g; Fat 0.7 g; Saturates 0.4 g

moderate

10 mins

35 mins

Fresh broad beans are best for this scrumptious soup, but if they are unavailable, use frozen beans instead.

Broad Bean *and* Mint Soup

1 Heat the olive oil in a large saucepan over a low heat. Add the onion and garlic and sauté for 2–3 minutes until softened.

2 Add the potatoes and cook, stirring constantly, for 5 minutes.

3 Stir in the beans and the vegetable stock, then cover the pan and simmer for 30 minutes or until the beans and potatoes are tender.

4 Remove a few vegetables with a slotted spoon and reserve. Place the remainder of the soup in a food processor or blender and process until you have a thoroughly smooth soup.

5 Return the soup to a clean saucepan and add the reserved vegetables and chopped mint. Stir thoroughly and heat through gently.

6 Transfer the soup to a warmed tureen or individual serving bowls. Garnish with swirls of yogurt and a few sprigs of fresh mint and serve immediately.

SERVES 4

2 tbsp olive oil
1 red onion, chopped
2 garlic cloves, crushed
450 g/1 lb potatoes, diced
500 g/1 lb 2 oz broad beans, thawed if frozen
850 ml/1½ pints vegetable stock
2 tbsp chopped fresh mint

to garnish
natural yogurt
fresh mint sprigs

NUTRITION
Calories *224*; Sugars *4 g*; Protein *12 g*; Carbohydrate *31 g*; Fat *6 g*; Saturates *1 g*

 very easy

15 mins

 40 mins

🥄 **COOK'S TIP**

Use fresh coriander and ½ teaspoon ground cumin as flavourings in the broad bean soup, if you prefer.

The combination of potato, garlic and onion works brilliantly in soup. In this recipe the garlic is roasted to give it added dimension and depth.

Roasted Garlic *and* Potato Soup

SERVES 4

1 large bulb of garlic with large cloves, peeled (about 100 g/3½ oz)
2 tsp olive oil, plus extra for brushing
2 large leeks, sliced thinly
1 large onion, chopped finely
500 g/1 lb 2 oz potatoes, diced
1.2 litres/2 pints chicken or vegetable stock
1 bay leaf
150 ml/5 fl oz single cream
freshly grated nutmeg
fresh lemon juice, optional
salt and pepper
snipped fresh chives, to garnish
crusty bread or toast, to serve

NUTRITION
Calories 240; Sugars 7 g; Protein 8 g;
Carbohydrate 33 g; Fat 10 g; Saturates 5 g

moderate

10 mins

1 hr

1 Put the garlic cloves into a baking dish, lightly brush with a little olive oil and bake in a preheated oven, 180°C/350°F/Gas Mark 4, for about 20 minutes until golden.

2 Heat the olive oil in a large saucepan over a medium heat. Add the leeks and onion, cover and cook for about 3 minutes, stirring frequently, until the vegetables begin to soften.

3 Add the potatoes, roasted garlic, stock and bay leaf. Season to taste with salt (unless the stock is salty already) and pepper. Bring to the boil, reduce the heat, cover and cook gently for about 30 minutes until the vegetables are tender. Remove and discard the bay leaf.

4 Leave the soup to cool slightly, then transfer to a food processor or blender and process until smooth, working in batches, if necessary. (If using a food processor, strain off the cooking liquid and reserve. Purée the soup solids with enough cooking liquid to moisten them, then combine with the remaining liquid.)

5 Return the soup to the saucepan and stir in the cream and a generous grating of nutmeg. Taste and adjust the seasoning, if necessary, adding a few drops of lemon juice, if wished. Reheat over a low heat. Ladle into warmed soup bowls, garnish with snipped chives and serve with crusty bread or toast.

Vichyssoise is simply cold leek and potato soup. The addition of watercress gives it a cool, refreshing flavour and lovely colour.

Watercress Vichyssoise

1 Heat the olive oil in a heavy-based saucepan over a medium heat. Add the thinly sliced leeks and cook gently for about 3 minutes, stirring frequently, until they begin to soften.

2 Add the potatoes, stock, water and bay leaf. Add salt if the stock is unsalted. Bring to the boil, then reduce the heat, cover the saucepan and cook gently for about 25 minutes until the vegetables are tender. Remove the bay leaf and discard.

3 Add the watercress and continue to cook for a further 2–3 minutes, stirring frequently, until the watercress is completely wilted.

4 Leave the soup to cool slightly, then transfer to a food processor or blender and process until smooth, working in batches, if necessary. (If using a food processor, strain off the cooking liquid and reserve. Purée the soup solids with enough cooking liquid to moisten them, then combine with the remaining liquid.)

5 Put the soup into a large bowl and then stir in half the cream. Season with salt, if needed, and plenty of pepper. Leave to cool to room temperature.

6 Leave to chill until cold. Taste and adjust the seasoning, if necessary. Ladle the watercress vichyssoise into chilled bowls, drizzle the remaining cream on top and garnish with watercress leaves. Serve immediately.

SERVES 6

1 tbsp olive oil
3 large leeks, sliced thinly
350 g/12 oz potatoes, diced finely
600 ml/1 pint chicken or vegetable stock
450 ml/16 fl oz water
1 bay leaf
175 g/6 oz prepared watercress
175 ml/6 fl oz single cream
salt and pepper
watercress leaves, to garnish

NUTRITION
Calories 42; Sugars 0.8 g; Protein 2.1 g; Carbohydrate 3.6 g; Fat 2.2 g; Saturates 1 g

  very easy

  15 mins

35 mins

This soup makes a
marvellous late autumn
or winter starter. It has
a delicious texture and
cheerful golden colour.

Sweet Potato *and* Apple Soup

SERVES 6

1 tbsp butter
3 leeks, sliced thinly
1 large carrot, sliced thinly
600 g/1 lb 5 oz sweet potatoes, peeled
    and cubed
2 large, tart eating apples, peeled and cubed
1.2 litres/2 pints water
freshly grated nutmeg
225 ml/8 fl oz apple juice
225 ml/8 fl oz single cream
salt and pepper

to garnish
snipped fresh chives
bunches of fresh chives

1 Melt the butter in a large saucepan over a medium–low heat. Add the leeks, cover and cook for 6–8 minutes, or until softened stirring frequently.

2 Add the carrot, sweet potatoes, apples and water. Season lightly with salt, pepper and nutmeg. Bring to the boil, reduce the heat and simmer, covered, for 20 minutes, stirring occasionally, until the vegetables are very tender.

3 Leave the soup to cool slightly, then transfer to a food processor or blender and process until smooth, working in batches, if necessary. (If using a food processor, strain off the cooking liquid and reserve. Purée the soup solids with enough cooking liquid to moisten them, then combine with the remaining liquid.)

4 Return the puréed soup to the saucepan and stir in the apple juice. Place over a low heat and simmer for about 10 minutes until heated through.

5 Stir in the cream and continue simmering for 5 minutes, stirring frequently, until heated through. Taste and adjust the seasoning, adding more salt, pepper and nutmeg, if necessary. Ladle the soup into warmed bowls, garnish with snipped chives and a few bunches of fresh chives, then serve.

NUTRITION

Calories 57; Sugars 3.8 g; Protein 0.7 g;
Carbohydrate 7.4 g; Fat 2.9 g; Saturates 1.8 g

moderate

10 mins

45 mins

This is a classic creamy soup made from potatoes and leeks. To achieve the delicate pale colour, be sure to use only the white parts of the leeks.

Vichyssoise

1 Trim the leeks and remove the green parts. Using a sharp knife, slice the white parts of the leeks very finely.

2 Melt the butter or margarine in a saucepan over a low heat. Add the leeks and onion and fry, stirring occasionally, for 5 minutes without browning.

3 Add the potatoes, vegetable stock, lemon juice, nutmeg, coriander and bay leaf to the pan, season to taste with salt and pepper and bring to the boil. Cover and simmer for 30 minutes until all the vegetables are very soft.

4 Leave the soup to cool slightly, remove and discard the bay leaf and then press through a sieve or process in a food processor or blender until smooth. Pour the soup into a clean pan.

5 Blend the egg yolk into the cream, add a little of the soup to the egg mixture and then whisk it back into the soup and reheat gently, without boiling. Taste and adjust the seasoning, if necessary. Leave to cool and then chill thoroughly in the refrigerator.

6 Ladle the chilled soup into large soup bowls, garnish with snipped chives and a handful of fresh chives, then serve.

SERVES 4

3 large leeks
3 tbsp butter or margarine
1 onion, sliced thinly
500 g/1 lb 2 oz potatoes, chopped
850 ml/1½ pints vegetable stock
2 tsp lemon juice
pinch of ground nutmeg
¼ tsp ground coriander
1 bay leaf
1 egg yolk
150 ml/5 fl oz single cream
salt and pepper

to garnish
snipped fresh chives
handful of fresh chives

NUTRITION
Calories *208*; Sugars *5 g*; Protein *5 g*;
Carbohydrate *20 g*; Fat *12 g*; Saturates *6 g*

⭐ very easy
◔ 10 mins
🕐 40 mins

This chunky, aromatic soup is perfect for a cold-weather lunch or supper served with crusty bread and a salad, if wished.

Smoked Haddock Soup

SERVES 4

1 tbsp oil
55 g/2 oz smoked streaky bacon, cut into matchsticks
1 large onion, chopped finely
2 tbsp plain flour
1 litre/1³/₄ pints milk
700 g/1 lb 9 oz potatoes, cubed
175 g/6 oz skinless smoked haddock
salt and pepper
finely chopped fresh parsley, to garnish

1 Heat the oil in a large saucepan over a medium heat. Add the bacon and cook for 2 minutes. Stir in the onion and continue cooking for 5–7 minutes, stirring frequently, until the onion is soft and the bacon golden. Tip the pan and spoon off as much fat as possible.

2 Stir in the flour and continue cooking for 2 minutes. Add half of the milk and stir well, scraping the base of the pan to mix in the flour.

3 Add the potatoes and remaining milk and season with pepper. Bring just to the boil, stirring frequently, then reduce the heat and simmer, partially covered, for 10 minutes.

4 Add the smoked haddock and continue cooking, stirring occasionally, for 15 minutes or until the potatoes are tender and the fish breaks up easily.

5 Taste the soup and adjust the seasoning, if necessary (salt may not be needed). Ladle into a warmed tureen or 4 large soup bowls and garnish with a sprinkling of chopped parsley.

NUTRITION
Calories *80*; Sugars *2.9 g*; Protein *4.3 g*;
Carbohydrate *9.6 g*; Fat *3 g*; Saturates *1.4 g*

easy
5–10 mins
40 mins

 COOK'S TIP

Cutting the potatoes into small cubes not only looks attractive, it allows them to cook more quickly and evenly.

Fishermen's soups are variable, depending on the season and the catch. Monkfish has a texture like lobster, but tender cod is equally appealing.

Breton Fish Soup *with* Cider

1 Melt the butter in a large saucepan over a medium-low heat. Add the leek and shallots and cook for about 5 minutes, stirring frequently, until they begin to soften. Add the cider and bring to the boil.

2 Stir in the fish stock, potatoes and bay leaf with a large pinch of salt (unless the stock is already quite salty) and bring back to the boil. Reduce the heat, cover and cook gently for 10 minutes.

3 Put the flour into a small bowl and very slowly whisk in a few tablespoons of the milk to make a thick paste. Stir in a little more milk, if needed, to make a smooth liquid.

4 Adjust the heat so that the soup bubbles gently. Stir in the flour mixture and cook, stirring frequently, for 5 minutes. Add the remaining milk and half the cream. Continue cooking for about 10 minutes until the potatoes are tender.

5 Combine the sorrel with the remaining cream. (If using a food processor, add the sorrel and chop, then add the cream and process briefly.)

6 Stir the sorrel cream into the soup and add the fish. Continue cooking, stirring occasionally, for 3 minutes or until the monkfish stiffens or the cod just begins to flake. Taste the soup and adjust the seasoning, if necessary. Ladle into 4 warmed soup bowls and serve.

S E R V E S   4

2 tsp butter
1 large leek, sliced thinly
2 shallots, chopped finely
300 ml/10 fl oz cider
125 ml/4 fl oz fish stock
250 g/9 oz potatoes, diced
1 bay leaf
4 tbsp plain flour
175 ml/6 fl oz milk
175 ml/6 fl oz double cream
55 g/2 oz fresh sorrel leaves, chopped finely
350 g/12 oz skinless monkfish or cod fillet, cut into 2.5-cm/1-inch pieces
salt and pepper

N U T R I T I O N

Calories *103*; Sugars *1.5 g*; Protein *5.2 g*; Carbohydrate *6.6 g*; Fat *6.3 g*; Saturates *3.8 g*

easy

5–10 mins

 40 mins

This light and refreshing soup is also good served cold. An ideal starter for a summer meal, served with crunchy Melba toast.

Fennel *and* Tomato Soup

S E R V E S   4

2 tsp olive oil
1 large onion, halved and sliced
2 large fennel bulbs, halved and sliced
1 small potato, diced
850 ml/1½ pints water
400 ml/14 fl oz tomato juice
1 bay leaf
125 g/4½ oz cooked small prawns, peeled
2 tomatoes, peeled, deseeded and chopped
½ tsp snipped fresh dill
salt and pepper
sprigs of fresh dill or fennel fronds, to garnish

1 Heat the olive oil in a large saucepan over a medium heat. Add the sliced onion and fennel and cook for 3–4 minutes, stirring occasionally.

2 Add the potato, water, tomato juice and bay leaf with a large pinch of salt. Reduce the heat, cover and simmer for about 25 minutes, stirring once or twice, until the vegetables are soft.

3 Leave the soup to cool slightly, then transfer to a food processor or blender and process until smooth, working in batches, if necessary. (If using a food processor, strain off the cooking liquid and reserve. Purée the soup solids with enough cooking liquid to moisten them, then combine with the remaining liquid.)

4 Return the soup to the saucepan and add the prawns. Simmer gently for 10 minutes, to reheat the soup and allow it to absorb the prawn flavour.

5 Stir in the tomatoes and dill. Taste and adjust the seasoning, adding salt, if needed, and pepper. Thin the soup with a little more tomato juice, if wished. Ladle into warmed bowls, garnish with dill sprigs or fennel fronds and serve.

N U T R I T I O N
Calories *110*; Sugars *8 g*; Protein *10 g*;
Carbohydrate *13 g*; Fat *2 g*; Saturates *0 g*

⭐   very easy
🕐   30 mins
🕐   40 mins

This is a traditional, creamy Scottish soup. As the smoked haddock has quite a strong flavour, it has been mixed with some fresh cod.

Cullen Skink

1 Put the haddock fillet into a large frying pan and cover with boiling water. Leave for 10 minutes. Drain, reserving 300 ml/10 fl oz of the soaking water. Flake the fish, taking care to remove all the bones.

2 Heat the butter in a large saucepan over a low heat. Add the onion and cook gently for 10 minutes until softened. Add the milk and bring to a gentle simmer before adding the potatoes. Cook for 10 minutes.

3 Add the reserved haddock flakes and cod. Simmer for a further 10 minutes until the cod is tender.

4 Remove about one-third of the fish and potatoes, put into a food processor and process until smooth. Alternatively, rub through a sieve into a bowl. Return to the soup with the cream, parsley and seasoning. Taste and add a little lemon juice, if wished. Add a little of the reserved soaking water if the soup seems too thick. Reheat gently. Ladle the soup into 4 large, warmed soup bowls, garnish with lemon slices and a few sprigs of fresh parsley. Serve immediately.

SERVES 4

225 g/8 oz undyed smoked haddock fillet
2 tbsp butter
1 onion, chopped finely
600 ml/1 pint milk
350 g/12 oz potatoes, diced
350 g/12 oz cod, boned, skinned and cubed
150 ml/5 fl oz double cream
2 tbsp chopped fresh parsley
lemon juice, to taste
salt and pepper

to garnish
lemon slices
fresh parsley sprigs

NUTRITION
Calories *108*; Sugars *2.3 g*; Protein *7.4 g*;
Carbohydrate *5.6 g*; Fat *6.4 g*; Saturates *3.9 g*

⭐⭐⭐ moderate
🕐 20 mins
🕐 40 mins

 COOK'S TIP

Look for Finnan haddock, if you can find it. If unavailable, use undyed haddock, but try not to use yellow-dyed haddock fillet.

This hearty soup of beans and vegetables is from Nice and gets its name from the fresh basil sauce which is stirred in at the last minute.

Pistou

SERVES 4

2 young carrots
450 g/1 lb potatoes
200 g/7 oz fresh peas in their shells
200 g/7 oz thin French beans
150 g/5½ oz young courgettes
2 tbsp olive oil
1 garlic clove, crushed
1 large onion, chopped finely
2.5 litres/4½ pints vegetable stock or water
1 bouquet garni of 2 sprigs of fresh parsley
    and 1 bay leaf tied in a 7.5-cm/3-inch
    piece of celery
85 g/3 oz dried small soup pasta
1 large tomato, peeled, deseeded and
    chopped or diced
fresh Parmesan cheese shavings, to serve

pistou sauce
75 g/2¾ oz fresh basil leaves
1 garlic clove
5 tbsp fruity extra virgin olive oil
salt and pepper

NUTRITION
Calories 55; Sugars 1.2 g; Protein 3.8 g;
Carbohydrate 4.2 g; Fat 2.6 g; Saturates 0.6 g

easy

10 mins

25 mins

1 To make the pistou sauce, put the basil leaves, garlic and olive oil into a food processor and process until well blended. Season to taste with salt and pepper. Transfer to a bowl, cover with clingfilm and chill until required.

2 Peel the carrots and cut them in half lengthways, then slice. Peel the potatoes and cut into quarters lengthways, then slice. Leave to stand in a bowl of water until ready to use, to prevent discoloration.

3 Shell the peas. Top and tail the French beans and cut them into 2.5-cm/ 1-inch pieces. Cut the courgettes in half lengthways, then slice.

4 Heat the olive oil in a saucepan or flameproof casserole over a low heat. Add the garlic and fry for 2 minutes, stirring. Add the onion and fry for 2 minutes until softened. Add the carrots and potatoes and stir for 30 seconds.

5 Pour in the stock and bring to the boil. Reduce the heat, partially cover and simmer for 8 minutes, until the vegetables are beginning to become tender.

6 Stir in the peas, beans, courgettes, bouquet garni and pasta. Season to taste and cook for 4 minutes or until the vegetables and pasta are tender. Stir in the pistou sauce and serve with shavings of Parmesan cheese.

This mildly spiced, rich green soup is delicately scented with ginger and lemon grass. It makes a good light starter or summer lunch dish.

Spinach *and* Ginger Soup

1 Heat the sunflower oil in a large saucepan over a low heat. Add the onion, garlic and ginger, and fry for 3–4 minutes until softened, but not browned.

2 Reserve 2–3 small spinach leaves. Add the remaining leaves and lemon grass to the saucepan, stirring until the spinach is wilted. Add the stock and potatoes to the pan and bring to the boil. Reduce the heat, cover and simmer for about 10 minutes.

3 Tip the soup into a food processor or blender and process until smooth.

4 Return the soup to the pan and add the Chinese rice wine, then adjust the seasoning to taste with salt and pepper. Heat until just about to boil.

5 Finely shred the 2–3 reserved spinach leaves and scatter some over the top. Drizzle with a few drops of sesame oil and serve hot, garnished with the finely shredded fresh spinach leaves.

SERVES 4

2 tbsp sunflower oil
1 onion, chopped
2 garlic cloves, chopped finely
2 tsp finely chopped fresh root ginger
250 g/9 oz fresh young spinach leaves
1 small lemon grass stalk, chopped finely
1 litre/1³/₄ pints chicken or vegetable stock
225 g/8 oz potatoes, chopped
1 tbsp Chinese rice wine or dry sherry
1 tsp sesame oil
salt and pepper
fresh spinach, shredded finely, to garnish

NUTRITION
Calories *38*; Sugars *0.8 g*; Protein *3.2 g*;
Carbohydrate *2.4 g*; Fat *1.8 g*; Saturates *0.2 g*

 easy

 5–10 mins

25 mins

🎩 COOK'S TIP

To make a creamy-textured spinach and coconut soup, stir in 4 tablespoons creamed coconut, or replace about 300 ml/10 fl oz of the stock with coconut milk. Scatter with shavings of fresh coconut.

This soup makes a festive seafood extravaganza worthy of any special occasion or celebration.

Bouillabaisse

SERVES 6

450 g/1 lb tiger prawns
750 g/1 lb 10 oz firm white fish fillets,
    such as sea bass, snapper and monkfish
4 tbsp olive oil
grated rind of 1 orange
1 large garlic clove, chopped finely
½ tsp chilli paste or harissa
1 large leek, sliced
1 onion, halved and sliced
1 red pepper, deseeded and sliced
3–4 tomatoes, cored and cut into eighths
4 garlic cloves, sliced
1 bay leaf
pinch of saffron threads
½ tsp fennel seeds
600 ml/1 pint water
1.2 litres/2 pints fish stock
1 fennel bulb, chopped finely
1 large onion, chopped finely
225 g/8 oz potatoes, halved and thinly sliced
250 g/9 oz scallops
salt and pepper
toasted French bread and aïoli, to serve

NUTRITION

Calories 55; Sugars 1.1 g; Protein 7.2 g;
Carbohydrate 2.6 g; Fat 1.8 g; Saturates 0.3 g

moderate

10 mins

1 hr 5 mins

1 Peel the prawns and reserve the shells. Cut the fish fillets into serving pieces about 5 cm/2 inches square. Trim off any ragged edges and reserve. Put the fish in a bowl with 2 tablespoons of the olive oil, the orange rind, garlic and chilli paste or harissa. Turn to coat well, cover and leave to chill in the refrigerator. Chill the prawns and fish separately.

2 Heat 1 tablespoon of the olive oil in a large saucepan over a medium heat. Add the leek, sliced onion and red pepper. Cover and cook for 5 minutes, stirring, until the onion softens. Stir in the tomatoes, sliced garlic, bay leaf, saffron, fennel seeds, prawn shells, water and fish stock. Bring to the boil, then simmer, covered, for 30 minutes. Strain the fish stock and reserve.

3 Heat the remaining olive oil in a large pan. Add the fennel and chopped onion and cook for 5 minutes, stirring, until softened. Add the reserved stock and potatoes and bring to the boil. Reduce the heat slightly, cover and cook for about 12–15 minutes until just tender.

4 Reduce the heat and add the chilled fish, beginning with thick pieces and adding thinner ones after 2–3 minutes. Add the chilled prawns and scallops and continue simmering gently until all the seafood is cooked and opaque.

5 Taste the soup and adjust the seasoning, if necessary. Ladle into 6 large, warmed soup bowls. Spread the aïoli on the toasted bread slices and arrange on top of the soup.

This soup can be made in stages, so it is ideal for entertaining because some of it can be prepared in advance.

Mussel *and* Potato Soup

1 Discard any broken mussels and those with open shells that do not close when tapped. Wash them under cold running water, pull off any 'beards' and scrape off barnacles with a knife. Put the mussels into a large heavy-based saucepan. Cover tightly and cook over a high heat for about 4 minutes or until the mussels are open.

2 When cool enough to handle, remove the mussels from the shells, adding any additional juices to the cooking liquid. Strain the cooking liquid into a bowl through a muslin-lined sieve and reserve.

3 Put the flour into a bowl and very slowly whisk in a few tablespoons of the milk to form a thick paste. Stir in a little more to make a smooth liquid.

4 Put the remaining milk, cream and garlic into a saucepan and bring to the boil. Whisk in the flour mixture. Reduce the heat to medium–low and simmer for about 15 minutes or until the garlic is tender and the liquid has thickened slightly. Drop in the parsley leaves and cook for 2–3 minutes.

5 Leave the soup base to cool slightly, then process in a blender until smooth.

6 Return the soup to the saucepan and stir in the mussel cooking liquid and the potatoes. Season to taste with salt, if needed, and pepper. Simmer the soup gently for 5–7 minutes until reheated. Add the mussels and continue cooking for about 2 minutes until the soup is steaming and the mussels are hot. Ladle the soup into 4 warmed bowls and garnish with lemon slices and a few sprigs of fresh dill. Serve.

SERVES 4

1 kg/2 lb 4 oz mussels
3 tbsp plain flour
600 ml/1 pint milk
300 ml/10 fl oz whipping cream
1–2 garlic cloves, chopped finely
1 large bunch of curly parsley leaves
300 g/10½ oz cooked potatoes, diced
salt and pepper

to garnish
lemon slices
fresh dill sprigs

NUTRITION
Calories *95*; Sugars *1.8 g*; Protein *3.7 g*;
Carbohydrate *6.4 g*; Fat *6.2 g*; Saturates *3.7 g*

easy

15 mins

45 mins

The potato has been part of the Irish diet for centuries. This recipe is originally from the beautiful area of Moira, Northern Ireland.

Tom's Chicken Soup

SERVES 4

3 smoked bacon rashers, chopped
500 g/1 lb 2 oz skinless, boneless chicken, chopped
2 tbsp butter
675 g/1 lb 8 oz potatoes, chopped
3 onions, chopped
600 ml/1 pint giblet or chicken stock
600 ml/1 pint milk
150 ml/5 fl oz double cream
2 tbsp chopped fresh parsley
salt and pepper
soda bread, to serve

1 Gently fry the bacon and chicken in a large saucepan over a low heat for about 10 minutes.

2 Add the butter, potatoes and onions and cook for 15 minutes, stirring.

3 Add the stock and the milk, then bring the soup to the boil and simmer for 45 minutes. Season to taste with salt and pepper.

4 Pour in the cream and blend into the soup. Simmer gently over a low heat for 5 minutes. Add the chopped fresh parsley, then transfer the soup to a warmed tureen or individual bowls and serve with soda bread.

NUTRITION
Calories 97; Sugars 1.8 g; Protein 7.3 g; Carbohydrate 4.2 g; Fat 2 g; Saturates 3.3 g

⭐ very easy
🕐 5 mins
🕐 1 hr 20 mins

 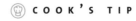 COOK'S TIP

Soda bread is made with bicarbonate of soda as the raising agent. It can be made with plain flour or wholemeal flour.

This creamy soup is filled with chunky vegetables and aromatic herbs. Using baby vegetables gives the soup an attractive look.

Chicken *and* Vegetable Soup

1 Put the stock into a saucepan with the chicken, parsley and tarragon sprigs and garlic. Bring just to the boil, reduce the heat, cover and simmer for 20 minutes or until the chicken is cooked through and firm to the touch.

2 Remove the chicken and strain the stock. When the chicken is cool enough to handle, cut into bite-sized pieces and reserve until required.

3 Return the stock to the saucepan and bring to the boil. Adjust the heat so the liquid boils very gently. Add the carrots, cover and cook for 5 minutes. Add the potatoes, cover again and cook for about 12 minutes or until the vegetables are beginning to become tender.

4 Meanwhile, put the flour into a small mixing bowl and very slowly whisk in the milk to make a thick paste. Pour in a little of the hot stock mixture and stir well to make a smooth liquid.

5 Stir the flour mixture into the soup and bring just to the boil, stirring. Boil gently for 4–5 minutes until it thickens, stirring frequently.

6 Add the spring onions, asparagus and chicken. Reduce the heat slightly and simmer for about 15 minutes until all the vegetables are tender. Stir in the cream and herbs. Season to taste with salt and pepper and serve.

SERVES 4

1 litre/1¾ pints chicken stock
175 g/6 oz skinless, boneless chicken breast
fresh parsley and tarragon sprigs
2 garlic cloves, crushed
125 g/4½ oz baby carrots, halved or quartered
225 g/8 oz small new potatoes, quartered
4 tbsp plain flour
125 ml/4 fl oz milk
4–5 spring onions, sliced diagonally
85 g/3 oz asparagus tips, halved and cut into 4-cm/1½-inch pieces
125 ml/4 fl oz whipping or double cream
1 tbsp finely chopped fresh parsley
1 tbsp finely chopped fresh tarragon
salt and pepper

NUTRITION
Calories 77; Sugars 1.5 g; Protein 5.5 g; Carbohydrate 6.9 g; Fat 3.3 g; Saturates 1.9 g

⭐⭐   easy

🕐   5 mins

🕐   1 hr

Leek and potato soup is a classic recipe. Here the soup is enhanced with smoked bacon pieces and enriched with double cream for a little luxury.

Leek, Potato *and* Bacon Soup

SERVES 4

25 g/1 oz butter
175 g/6 oz potatoes, diced
4 leeks, shredded
2 garlic cloves, crushed
100 g/3½ oz smoked bacon, diced
850 ml/1½ pints vegetable stock
225 ml/8 fl oz double cream
2 tbsp chopped fresh parsley
salt and pepper

to garnish
600 ml/1 pint vegetable oil
1 leek, shredded

1 Melt the butter in a large saucepan over a low heat. Add the potatoes, leeks, garlic and bacon. Sauté gently for 5 minutes, stirring constantly.

2 Add the vegetable stock and bring to the boil. Reduce the heat, cover the saucepan and simmer for 20 minutes until the potatoes are cooked. Stir in the cream and mix well.

3 Meanwhile, make the garnish. Half-fill a pan with vegetable oil and heat to 180°–190°C/350°–375°F, or until a cube of bread browns in 30 seconds. Add the shredded leek and deep-fry for 1 minute until browned and crisp, taking care because it contains water and this will make the oil spatter. Drain the shredded leek thoroughly on kitchen paper and reserve.

4 Reserve a few pieces of potato, leek and bacon. Put the rest of the soup into a food processor or blender, in batches, and process each batch for about 30 seconds. Return the puréed soup to a clean saucepan and heat through gently, stirring.

5 Stir in the reserved vegetables, bacon and parsley and season to taste with salt and pepper. Ladle into 4 warmed bowls and garnish with the fried leeks.

NUTRITION
Calories 93; Sugars 1 g; Protein 3.3 g;
Carbohydrate 2.7 g; Fat 7.8 g; Saturates 4.4 g

easy

5 mins

30 mins

🍴 **COOK'S TIP**

For a lighter soup, omit the cream and stir yogurt or crème fraîche into the soup at the end of the cooking time.

A comforting and satisfying cold weather soup, this is good served with bread as a light main course, but it is not too filling to be a starter soup.

Lentil, Potato *and* Ham Soup

1 Rinse and drain the lentils and remove any small stones, if necessary.

2 Melt the butter in a large saucepan or flameproof casserole over a medium heat. Add the onion, carrots and garlic, cover and cook for 4–5 minutes until the onion is slightly softened, stirring frequently.

3 Add the lentils with the water, bay leaf and sage or rosemary. Bring to the boil, reduce the heat, cover and simmer for 10 minutes.

4 Add the stock, potatoes, tomato purée and ham. Bring back to a simmer. Cover and continue simmering the soup for 25–30 minutes or until all the vegetables are tender.

5 Season to taste with salt and pepper, then remove and discard the bay leaf. Ladle into 4 warmed bowls, garnish with parsley and serve.

SERVES 4

300 g/10½ oz Puy lentils
2 tsp butter
1 large onion, chopped finely
2 carrots, chopped finely
1 garlic clove, chopped finely
450 ml/16 fl oz water
1 bay leaf
¼ tsp dried sage or rosemary
1 litre/1¾ pints chicken stock
225 g/8 oz potatoes, diced
1 tbsp tomato purée
115 g/4 oz smoked ham, diced finely
salt and pepper
chopped fresh parsley, to garnish

NUTRITION
Calories *61*; Sugars *1.4 g*; Protein *5.4 g*;
Carbohydrate *8.6 g*; Fat *0.8 g*; Saturates *0.3 g*

⭐⭐   easy

        10 mins

     45–50 mins

This is a real winter warmer – pieces of tender beef and chunky mixed vegetables are cooked in a stock which is flavoured with sherry.

Chunky Potato *and* Beef Soup

SERVES 4

2 tbsp vegetable oil
225 g/8 oz lean frying steak, cut into strips
225 g/8 oz new potatoes, halved
1 carrot, diced
2 celery sticks, sliced
2 leeks, sliced
850 ml/1½ pints beef stock
8 baby corn cobs, sliced
1 bouquet garni
2 tbsp dry sherry
salt and pepper
chopped fresh parsley, to garnish

1 Heat the vegetable oil in a large saucepan over a medium heat.

2 Add the meat to the saucepan and cook for 3 minutes, turning constantly.

3 Add the potatoes, carrot, celery and leeks. Cook for a further 5 minutes, stirring frequently.

4 Pour the beef stock into the saucepan and bring to the boil. Reduce the heat until the liquid is simmering, then add the sliced baby corn cobs and the bouquet garni.

5 Cook the soup for a further 20 minutes or until cooked through.

6 Remove the bouquet garni from the saucepan and discard. Stir the dry sherry into the soup and then season to taste with salt and pepper.

7 Ladle the soup into 4 warmed bowls and garnish with the chopped fresh parsley. Serve immediately.

NUTRITION
Calories 187; Sugars 3 g; Protein 14 g;
Carbohydrate 12 g; Fat 9 g; Saturates 2 g

easy

5 mins

35 mins

COOK'S TIP

Make double the quantity of soup and freeze the remainder in a rigid container for later use. When ready to use, leave in the refrigerator to thaw thoroughly, then heat until piping hot.

A thick and hearty soup, nourishing and substantial enough to serve as a main meal with wholemeal bread, if wished.

Indian Bean Soup

1 Heat the ghee or vegetable oil in a saucepan over a medium heat. Add all the prepared vegetables, except the courgettes and green pepper, and cook, stirring frequently, for 5 minutes. Add the garlic, ground coriander, paprika and curry paste and cook, stirring constantly, for 1 minute.

2 Stir in the stock and season with salt to taste. Bring to the boil, cover and simmer over a low heat, stirring occasionally, for 25 minutes.

3 Stir in the black-eyed beans, sliced courgettes and green pepper, then replace the lid and continue cooking for a further 15 minutes or until all the vegetables are tender.

4 Process 300 ml/10 fl oz of the soup mixture (about 2 ladlefuls) in a food processor or blender. Return the puréed mixture to the soup in the pan and reheat until piping hot. Sprinkle the soup with chopped coriander (if using) and serve hot.

SERVES 6

4 tbsp ghee or vegetable oil
2 onions, chopped
225 g/8 oz potatoes, cut into chunks
225 g/8 oz parsnips, cut into chunks
225 g/8 oz turnips or swedes, cut into chunks
2 celery sticks, sliced
2 courgettes, sliced
1 green pepper, deseeded and cut into 1-cm/1/2-inch pieces
2 garlic cloves, crushed
2 tsp ground coriander
1 tbsp paprika
1 tbsp mild curry paste
1.2 litres/2 pints vegetable stock
salt
400 g/14 oz canned black-eyed beans, drained and rinsed
chopped fresh coriander, to garnish (optional)

NUTRITION
Calories 237; Sugars 9 g; Protein 9 g;
Carbohydrate 33 g; Fat 9 g; Saturates 1 g

easy

20 mins

50 mins

Potato skins are always a favourite. Prepare the skins in advance and warm them through before serving with the salad fillings.

Potato Skins *and* Two Fillings

SERVES 4

4 large baking potatoes
2 tbsp vegetable oil
4 tsp salt
fresh chives, to garnish
150 ml/5 fl oz soured cream, to serve

beansprout filling

50 g/1¾ oz beansprouts
1 celery stick, sliced
1 orange, peeled and segmented
1 red eating apple, chopped
½ red pepper, deseeded and chopped
1 tbsp chopped fresh parsley
1 tbsp light soy sauce
1 tbsp clear honey
1 small garlic clove, crushed

bean filling

100 g/3½ oz canned mixed beans, drained
1 onion, halved and sliced
1 tomato, chopped
2 spring onions, chopped
2 tsp lemon juice
salt and pepper

NUTRITION

Calories 279; Sugars 2 g; Protein 5 g;
Carbohydrate 44 g; Fat 11 g; Saturates 7 g

        easy

30 mins

1 hr 10 mins

1 Scrub the potatoes and put on a baking tray. Prick the potatoes all over with a fork and rub the vegetable oil and salt into the skin.

2 Cook in a preheated oven, 200°C/400°F/Gas Mark 6, for 1 hour or until soft.

3 Cut the potatoes in half lengthways and scoop out the flesh, leaving a 1-cm/½-inch thick shell. Put the potato shells, skin side uppermost, into the oven for about 10 minutes until crisp.

4 Mix the ingredients for the beansprout filling in a bowl, tossing in the soy sauce, honey and garlic to coat.

5 Mix all the ingredients for the bean filling together in a separate bowl.

6 Mix the soured cream and chives together in a separate bowl until blended.

7 Fill the potato skins with the 2 salad fillings and garnish with fresh chives. Serve with the soured cream and chive sauce.

Use any mixture of beans you have to hand in this recipe, but the wider the variety, the more colourful the salad.

Mixed Bean *and* Apple Salad

1 Cook the quartered potatoes in a saucepan of boiling water for 15 minutes until tender. Drain and transfer to a mixing bowl.

2 Add the mixed beans to the potatoes, together with the apple, pepper, shallot and fennel. Mix well, taking care not to break up the potatoes.

3 To make the dressing, whisk all the dressing ingredients together until thoroughly combined, then pour it over the salad.

4 Line a serving plate or salad bowl with the oak-leaf lettuce leaves and spoon the salad mixture into the centre. Serve the salad immediately.

SERVES 4

225 g/8 oz new potatoes, scrubbed and quartered
225 g/8 oz mixed canned beans, such as red kidney beans, flageolet and borlotti beans, drained and rinsed
1 red eating apple, diced and tossed in 1 tbsp lemon juice
1 yellow pepper, deseeded and diced
1 shallot, sliced
½ fennel bulb, sliced
oak-leaf lettuce leaves

dressing
1 tbsp red wine vinegar
2 tbsp olive oil
½ tbsp American mustard
1 garlic clove, crushed
2 tsp chopped fresh thyme

NUTRITION
Calories *183*; Sugars *8 g*; Protein *6 g*;
Carbohydrate *26 g*; Fat *7 g*; Saturates *1 g*

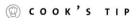 **COOK'S TIP**

Use Dijon or wholegrain mustard in place of American mustard, if you prefer.

⭐ very easy
🕐 20 mins
🕐 20 mins

POTATOES

The beetroot adds a rich colour to this dish. The dill dressing with the potatoes is a classic combination.

Beetroot Salad *and* Dill Dressing

SERVES 4

450 g/1 lb waxy potatoes, diced
4 small cooked beetroot, sliced
½ small cucumber, sliced thinly
2 large dill pickles, sliced
1 red onion, halved and sliced
fresh dill sprigs, to garnish

dressing
1 garlic clove, crushed
2 tbsp olive oil
2 tbsp red wine vinegar
2 tbsp chopped fresh dill
salt and pepper

1 Cook the potatoes in a saucepan of boiling water for 15 minutes or until tender. Drain and leave to cool.

2 When cool, mix the potatoes and beetroot together in a bowl, cover with clingfilm and reserve.

3 Line a salad platter with the slices of cucumber, dill pickles and red onion.

4 Spoon the potato and beetroot mixture into the centre of the platter.

5 Whisk all the dressing ingredients together in a small bowl, then pour the dressing over the salad.

6 Serve the potato and beetroot salad immediately (see Cook's Tip), garnished with fresh dill sprigs.

NUTRITION
Calories *174*; Sugars *8 g*; Protein *4 g*;
Carbohydrate *27 g*; Fat *6 g*; Saturates *1 g*

  very easy

25 mins

15 mins

 COOK'S TIP

If making the salad in advance, do not mix the beetroot and potatoes until just before serving, because the beetroot will bleed its colour.

This hot fruity salad combines sweet potatoes and fried bananas with colourful mixed peppers, which are then tossed in a honey-based dressing.

Sweet Potato Salad

1 Cook the sweet potatoes in a saucepan of boiling water for 10–15 minutes until tender. Drain thoroughly and reserve.

2 Meanwhile, melt the butter in a frying pan over a low heat. Add the lemon juice, garlic and peppers and cook, stirring constantly, for 3 minutes.

3 Add the banana slices to the frying pan and cook for 1 minute. Remove the bananas from the pan with a slotted spoon and stir into the potatoes.

4 To make the croûtons, add the bread cubes to the frying pan and cook, stirring frequently, for 2 minutes, until they are golden-brown on all sides.

5 Mix the dressing ingredients together in a small saucepan and heat until the honey is runny.

6 Spoon the potato mixture into a serving dish and season to taste with salt and pepper. Pour the dressing over the potatoes and sprinkle the croûtons over the top. Serve immediately.

SERVES 4

500 g/1 lb 2 oz sweet potatoes, diced
55 g/2 oz butter
1 tbsp lemon juice
1 garlic clove, crushed
1 red pepper, deseeded and diced
1 green pepper, deseeded and diced
2 bananas, sliced thickly
2 thick slices white bread, crusts removed, diced
salt and pepper

dressing
2 tbsp clear honey
2 tbsp snipped chives
2 tbsp lemon juice
2 tbsp olive oil

NUTRITION

Calories *424*; Sugars *29 g*; Protein *5 g*; Carbohydrate *68 g*; Fat *17 g*; Saturates *8 g*

⭐⭐   easy
🍴   15 mins
🕐   20 mins

👑 COOK'S TIP

Use firm, slightly underripe bananas in this recipe because they won't turn soft and mushy when they are fried.

There are many hot, spicy, Indian potato dishes that are served with curry, but this fruity salad is delicious served chilled.

Indian Potato Salad

SERVES 4

900 g/2 lb floury potatoes, diced
75 g/2³⁄₄ oz small broccoli florets
1 small mango, diced
4 spring onions, sliced
salt and pepper
small cooked spiced poppadoms, to serve

dressing
¹⁄₂ tsp ground cumin
¹⁄₂ tsp ground coriander
1 tbsp mango chutney
150 ml/5 fl oz low-fat natural yogurt
1 tsp chopped fresh root ginger
2 tbsp chopped fresh coriander

1 Cook the potatoes in a saucepan of boiling water for 10 minutes or until tender. Drain and place in a mixing bowl.

2 Meanwhile, blanch the broccoli florets in a separate saucepan of boiling water for 2 minutes. Thoroughly drain the broccoli and add to the potatoes in the bowl.

3 When the potatoes and broccoli have cooled, add the mango and spring onions. Season to taste with salt and pepper and mix well to combine.

4 Stir all of the dressing ingredients together in a small bowl.

5 Spoon the dressing over the potato mixture and mix together carefully, taking care not to break up the potatoes and broccoli.

6 Serve the salad immediately with the spiced poppadoms.

NUTRITION
Calories *175*; Sugars *8 g*; Protein *6 g*;
Carbohydrate *38 g*; Fat *1 g*; Saturates *0.3 g*

 easy

25 mins

20 mins

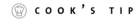 **COOK'S TIP**

Mix the dressing ingredients together in advance and leave to chill in the refrigerator for a few hours for a stronger flavour to develop.

Crisp fried potato nests make perfect edible salad bowls and are delicious when filled with a Chinese-style salad of vegetables and fruit.

Nests *of* Chinese Salad

1 To make the nests, rinse the grated potatoes several times in cold water. Drain well on kitchen paper so that they are completely dry. This is to prevent the potatoes from spitting when they are cooked in the fat. Place the potatoes in a mixing bowl. Add the cornflour and mix well to coat.

2 Half fill a preheated wok with vegetable oil and heat until smoking. Line a 15-cm/6-inch diameter wire sieve with one-quarter of the potato mixture and press another sieve of the same size on top.

3 Carefully lower the sieves into the oil and cook for 2 minutes until the potato nest is golden-brown and crisp. Remove the sieves from the wok, allowing the excess oil to drain off.

4 Repeat 3 more times to use up all of the grated potato mixture and make a total of 4 nests. Leave to cool.

5 Mix the salad ingredients together, then spoon into the potato nests.

6 To make the dressing, mix all of the dressing ingredients together. Pour the dressing over the salad, garnish with chives and serve immediately.

SERVES 4

potato nests
450 g/1 lb floury potatoes, grated
125 g/4½ oz cornflour
600 ml/1 pint vegetable oil, for frying
fresh chives, to garnish

salad
125 g/4½ oz pineapple, cubed
1 green pepper, cut into strips
1 carrot, cut into matchsticks
50 g/1¾ oz mangetouts, sliced thickly
4 baby corn cobs, halved lengthways
25 g/1 oz beansprouts
2 spring onions, sliced

dressing
1 tbsp clear honey
1 tsp light soy sauce
1 garlic clove, crushed
1 tsp lemon juice

NUTRITION
Calories *272*; Sugars *11 g*; Protein *4 g*;
Carbohydrate *59 g*; Fat *4 g*; Saturates *0.4 g*

 moderate

15 mins

15 mins

This green and white salad is made with creamy, salty goat's cheese – its distinctive flavour is perfect with salad leaves.

Potato, Rocket *and* Apple Salad

SERVES 4

600 g/1 lb 5 oz potatoes, unpeeled and sliced
2 green eating apples, diced
1 tsp lemon juice
25 g/1 oz walnut pieces
125 g/4½ oz goat's cheese, cubed
150 g/5½ oz rocket leaves
salt and pepper

dressing
2 tbsp olive oil
1 tbsp red wine vinegar
1 tsp clear honey
1 tsp fennel seeds

1 Cook the potatoes in a saucepan of boiling water for 15 minutes until tender. Drain and leave to cool. Transfer the cooled potatoes to a serving bowl.

2 Toss the diced apples in the lemon juice, then drain and stir them into the cold potatoes.

3 Add the walnut pieces, goat's cheese cubes and rocket leaves, then toss the ingredients together to mix. Season to taste with salt and pepper.

4 Whisk all of the dressing ingredients together in a small bowl and then pour the dressing over the salad and serve.

NUTRITION

Calories *104*; Sugars *3.1 g*; Protein *3.1 g*; Carbohydrate *12 g*; Fat *5.3 g*; Saturates *1.5 g*

easy
20 mins
15 mins

 COOK'S TIP

Serve this salad immediately to prevent the apple from discolouring. Alternatively, prepare all of the other ingredients in advance and add the apple at the last minute.

Grilled new potatoes are tossed in oil to give them a chargrilled flavour and colour. The salad is served warm with a garlic mayonnaise.

Grilled New Potato Salad

1 Cook the new potatoes in a saucepan of boiling water for 10 minutes. Drain.

2 Mix the olive oil, thyme and paprika together and pour the mixture over the warm potatoes.

3 Place the bacon rashers under a preheated medium-hot grill and cook for 5 minutes, turning once until crisp. When cooked, roughly chop the bacon and keep warm.

4 Transfer the potatoes to the grill pan and cook for 10 minutes, turning once.

5 Mix the dressing ingredients together in a bowl. Transfer the potatoes and bacon to a large serving bowl. Season to taste with salt and pepper and mix.

6 Spoon over the dressing, garnish with a parsley sprig and serve immediately. Alternatively, leave to cool and serve chilled.

SERVES 4

650 g/1 lb 7 oz new potatoes, scrubbed
3 tbsp olive oil
2 tbsp chopped fresh thyme
1 tsp paprika
4 smoked bacon rashers
salt and pepper
fresh parsley sprig, to garnish

dressing
4 tbsp mayonnaise
1 tbsp garlic wine vinegar
2 garlic cloves, crushed
1 tbsp chopped fresh parsley

NUTRITION
Calories *162*; Sugars *1 g*; Protein *3.2 g*;
Carbohydrate *12 g*; Fat *11.4 g*; Saturates *2.2 g*

easy

5 mins

25 mins

 COOK'S TIP

Add spicy sausage to the salad instead of bacon – you do not need to cook it under the grill before adding it to the salad.

This is a classic version of the French Salade Niçoise. It is a substantial salad, suitable for a lunch or light summer supper.

Tuna Niçoise Salad

SERVES 4

4 eggs
450 g/1 lb new potatoes
115 g/4 oz small French beans, trimmed and halved
2 tuna steaks, about 175 g/6 oz each
6 tbsp olive oil, plus extra for brushing
1 garlic clove, crushed
1½ tsp Dijon mustard
2 tsp lemon juice
2 tbsp chopped fresh basil
2 Little Gem lettuces
200 g/7 oz cherry tomatoes, halved
175 g/6 oz cucumber, peeled and sliced
50 g/1¾ oz stoned black olives
50 g/1¾ oz canned anchovy fillets in oil, drained
salt and pepper

NUTRITION
Calories 109; Sugars 1 g; Protein 7 g;
Carbohydrate 4.8 g; Fat 7 g; Saturates 1.2 g

 very easy

10 mins

20 mins

1 Bring a small saucepan of water to the boil over a medium heat. Add the eggs and cook for 7–9 minutes from when the water returns to a boil – 7 minutes for a slightly soft centre, or 9 minutes for a firm centre. Drain and refresh under cold running water. Set the hard-boiled eggs aside.

2 Cook the potatoes in boiling salted water for 10–12 minutes until tender. Add the French beans 3 minutes before the end of the cooking time. Drain both vegetables well and refresh under cold running water. Drain well.

3 Wash the tuna steaks under cold running water and pat dry with kitchen paper. Brush with a little olive oil and season to taste with salt and pepper. Cook on a preheated ridged griddle for 2–3 minutes on each side, until just tender, but still slightly pink in the centre. Reserve.

4 Whisk the garlic, mustard, lemon juice, basil and seasoning together. Whisk the olive oil into the dressing.

5 To assemble the salad, break apart the lettuces and tear into large pieces. Divide between 4 serving plates. Add the potatoes and beans, tomatoes, cucumber and olives. Toss lightly. Shell the eggs and cut into quarters lengthways. Arrange these on top of the salad. Scatter over the anchovies.

6 Flake the tuna and arrange on the salad. Pour over the dressing and serve.

The spicy peanut dressing served with this salad may be prepared in advance and left to chill a day before required.

Indonesian Chicken Salad

1 Using a sharp knife, carefully cut the potatoes into small cubes. Bring a large saucepan of water to the boil over a medium heat.

2 Cook the potatoes in the boiling water for 10 minutes or until tender.

3 Drain the diced potatoes and leave to cool. When cool, transfer the potatoes to a salad bowl.

4 Add the pineapple, carrots, beansprouts, spring onions, courgette, celery, peanuts and sliced chicken to the potatoes. Toss well to mix all the salad ingredients together thoroughly.

5 To make the dressing, put the peanut butter into a small mixing bowl and gradually whisk in the olive oil and soy sauce.

6 Stir in the red chilli, sesame oil and lime juice. Mix until well combined.

7 Pour the spicy dressing over the salad and toss lightly to coat all of the ingredients. Serve immediately.

SERVES 4

1.25 k/2 lb 12 oz waxy potatoes
300 g/10½ oz fresh pineapple, diced
2 carrots, grated
175 g/6 oz beansprouts
1 bunch of spring onions, sliced
1 large courgette, cut into matchsticks
3 celery sticks, cut into matchsticks
175 g/6 oz unsalted peanuts
2 cooked chicken breast fillets, about 125 g/4½ oz each, sliced

dressing
6 tbsp crunchy peanut butter
6 tbsp olive oil
2 tbsp light soy sauce
1 fresh red chilli, chopped
2 tsp sesame oil
4 tsp lime juice

NUTRITION
Calories *802*; Sugars *15 g*; Protein *35 g*; Carbohydrate *45 g*; Fat *55 g*; Saturates *10 g*

⭐⭐   easy
🕐   20 mins
🕐   15 mins

 COOK'S TIP

Unsweetened canned pineapple may be used instead of the fresh pineapple for convenience. If only sweetened canned pineapple is available, drain it and rinse under cold running water before using.

Tender chicken breast meat is perfect for salads. There is no wastage and the meat cooks quickly in small pieces, which are perfect for tossing.

Spicy Chicken Salad

SERVES 4

2 skinned chicken breast fillets, about
  125 g/4½ oz each
25 g/1 oz butter
1 fresh red chilli, chopped
1 tbsp clear honey
½ tsp ground cumin
2 tbsp chopped fresh coriander
600 g/1 lb 5 oz potatoes, diced
50 g/1¾ oz French beans, halved
1 red pepper, cut into thin strips
2 tomatoes, deseeded and diced

dressing
2 tbsp olive oil
pinch of chilli powder
1 tbsp garlic wine vinegar
pinch of caster sugar
1 tbsp chopped fresh coriander

1 Cut the chicken into thin strips. Melt the butter in a frying pan over a medium heat. Add the chicken, chilli, honey and cumin and cook for about 10 minutes, turning until cooked through.

2 Transfer the mixture to a bowl, leave to cool, then stir in the coriander.

3 Meanwhile, cook the diced potatoes in a large saucepan of boiling water for 10 minutes until tender. Drain well and leave to cool.

4 Blanch the French beans in a saucepan of boiling water for 3 minutes, then drain and leave to cool. Mix the French beans and potatoes together in a salad bowl.

5 Add the pepper and tomatoes to the potatoes and beans. Stir in the spicy chicken mixture, mixing to combine all the ingredients.

6 Whisk all of the dressing ingredients together in a small bowl and then pour the dressing over the salad, tossing well. Serve immediately.

NUTRITION
Calories *105*; Sugars *2.8 g*; Protein *6.7 g*;
Carbohydrate *9.2 g*; Fat *5 g*; Saturates *1.8 g*

⭐⭐ easy
🕐 20 mins
🕐 15 mins

 COOK'S TIP

If you prefer, use lean turkey meat instead of the chicken for a slightly stronger flavour. Use the white meat for the best appearance and flavour.

Sliced Italian sausage blends well with the other Mediterranean flavours of sun-dried tomato and basil in this salad.

Italian Sausage Salad

1 Cook the potatoes in a saucepan of boiling water for 20 minutes or until cooked through. Drain and leave to cool.

2 Line a large serving platter with the radicchio or lollo rosso lettuce leaves.

3 Slice the cooled potatoes and arrange them in layers on the lettuce-lined serving platter together with the sliced green pepper, sliced Italian sausage, red onion, sun-dried tomatoes and shredded fresh basil.

4 Put the balsamic vinegar, tomato purée and olive oil into a small bowl, then whisk together until thoroughly combined. Season to taste with salt and pepper. Pour the dressing over the potato salad and serve immediately.

SERVES 4

450 g/1 lb waxy potatoes
1 radicchio or lollo rosso lettuce
1 green pepper, sliced
175 g/6 oz Italian sausage, sliced
1 red onion, halved and sliced
125 g/4½ oz sun-dried tomatoes, sliced
2 tbsp shredded fresh basil

dressing
1 tbsp balsamic vinegar
1 tsp tomato purée
2 tbsp olive oil
salt and pepper

NUTRITION
Calories *450*; Sugars *6 g*; Protein *13 g*;
Carbohydrate *38 g*; Fat *28 g*; Saturates *1 g*

 easy

25 mins

 25 mins

COOK'S TIP

Any sliced Italian sausage or salami can be used in this salad. Italy is home of the salami and there are numerous varieties to choose from – those from the south tend to be more highly spiced than those from the north of the country.

Light Meals *and* Side Dishes

Potatoes are very versatile and can be used as a base to create an array of tempting light meals and satisfying snacks. They are also nutritious, and their carbohydrate gives a welcome energy boost. As potatoes have a fairly neutral flavour, they can be teamed with a variety of other ingredients and flavours. This section contains a range of delicious yet light meals – try Feta & Spinach Omelette, or Carrot & Potato Soufflé. Potatoes can be cooked in a variety of ways, such as mashing, roasting, deep-frying and baking, making them an adaptable component of any meal.

Crisp, twice-baked potatoes are partnered with an unusual filling of the Middle Eastern flavours of chickpeas, cumin and coriander.

Potatoes *with a* Spicy Filling

SERVES 4

4 large baking potatoes
1 tbsp vegetable oil, optional
430 g/15½ oz canned chickpeas, drained
1 tsp ground coriander
1 tsp ground cumin
4 tbsp chopped fresh coriander
150 ml/5 fl oz low-fat natural yogurt
salt and pepper

salad
2 tomatoes
½ cucumber
½ red onion

1 Scrub the potatoes and pat them dry with kitchen paper. Prick them all over with a fork, brush with oil (if using) and season with salt and pepper.

2 Place the potatoes on a large baking tray and bake in a preheated oven, 200°C/400°F/Gas Mark 6, for 1–1¼ hours or until cooked through. Leave the potatoes to cool for 10 minutes.

3 Meanwhile, put the chickpeas into a large bowl and mash with a fork or potato masher. Stir in the ground coriander, cumin and half the fresh coriander. Cover with clingfilm and reserve.

4 Halve the cooked potatoes and scoop the flesh into a bowl, keeping the shells intact. Mash the flesh until smooth and gently mix into the chickpea mixture with the yogurt. Season to taste with salt and pepper.

5 Place the potato shells on a baking tray and fill with the potato and chickpea mixture. Return the filled potatoes to the oven and bake for 10–15 minutes until thoroughly heated through.

6 Meanwhile, make the salad. Using a sharp knife, chop the tomatoes. Slice the cucumber and cut the red onion into thin slices. Toss all the ingredients together in a serving dish.

7 Serve the potatoes sprinkled with the remaining coriander and the salad.

NUTRITION
Calories 335; Sugars 7 g; Protein 15 g;
Carbohydrate 57 g; Fat 7 g; Saturates 1 g

very easy

20 mins

1 hr 30 mins

These Indian snacks are perfect for a quick or light meal, served with a salad. They can be made and frozen in advance for ease of use.

Vegetable Samosas

1 To make the filling, heat the vegetable oil in a frying pan over a low heat. Add the onion and sauté for 1–2 minutes until softened. Stir in all of the spices and garlic and cook for 1 minute until their aroma is released.

2 Add the diced potatoes to the frying pan and cook over a low heat, stirring frequently, for 5 minutes until they begin to soften.

3 Stir in the peas and spinach and cook for a further 3–4 minutes.

4 Lay the filo pastry sheets out on a clean work surface and carefully fold each sheet in half lengthways.

5 Place 2 tablespoons of the vegetable filling at one end of each folded pastry sheet. Fold over one corner to make a triangle. Continue folding in this way to make a triangular package and seal the edges with water.

6 Repeat with the remaining pastry and the remaining filling.

7 Heat the vegetable oil for deep-frying in a large saucepan or deep-fryer to 180°C/350°F or until a cube of bread browns in 30 seconds. Fry the samosas, in batches, for 1–2 minutes until golden. Drain on kitchen paper and keep warm while cooking the remainder. Serve the samosas immediately.

MAKES 12

filling
2 tbsp vegetable oil
1 onion, chopped
½ tsp ground coriander
½ tsp ground cumin
pinch of turmeric
½ tsp ground ginger
½ tsp garam masala
1 garlic clove, crushed
225 g/8 oz potatoes, diced
100 g/3½ oz frozen peas, thawed
150 g/5½ oz fresh spinach, chopped

pastry
350 g/12 oz (12 sheets) filo pastry
600 ml/1 pint vegetable oil, for deep-frying

NUTRITION
Calories *291*; Sugars *2 g*; Protein *4 g*;
Carbohydrate *18 g*; Fat *23 g*; Saturates *3 g*

⭐⭐⭐   moderate
     20 mins
     30 mins

These gnocchi, or small
dumplings, are made with
potato, flavoured with
spinach and nutmeg and
served in a delicious
tomato and basil sauce.

Gnocchi *with* Tomato Sauce

SERVES 4

450 g/1 lb baking potatoes
75 g/2 3/4 oz spinach
1 tsp water
40 g/1 1/2 oz butter or margarine
1 small egg, beaten
150 g/5 1/2 oz plain flour, plus extra
    for dusting
salt and pepper
fresh basil leaves, to garnish

tomato sauce

1 tbsp olive oil
1 shallot, chopped
1 tbsp tomato purée
225 g/8 oz canned chopped tomatoes
2 tbsp chopped fresh basil
6 tbsp red wine
1 tsp caster sugar

NUTRITION

Calories *337*; Sugars *4 g*; Protein *9 g*;
Carbohydrate *52 g*; Fat *10 g*; Saturates *4 g*

★★☆   moderate

🕑   25 mins

🕐   1 hr

1 Cook the potatoes in their skins in a saucepan of boiling salted water for
20 minutes. Drain well and press through a sieve into a bowl.

2 Cook the spinach in the water for 5 minutes or until wilted. Drain and pat
dry with kitchen paper, then chop and stir into the potatoes.

3 Add the butter or margarine, egg and half of the flour to the spinach
mixture, mixing well. Turn out on to a floured work surface, gradually
kneading in the remaining flour to form a soft dough.

4 With floured hands, roll the dough into thin ropes and cut off 2-cm/3/4-inch
pieces. Press the centre of each dumpling with your finger, drawing it
towards you to curl the sides of the gnocchi. Cover with clingfilm and leave
to chill in the refrigerator while you make the sauce.

5 Heat the olive oil for the sauce in a saucepan over a low heat. Add the
chopped shallots and sauté for 5 minutes. Add the tomato purée, tomatoes,
basil, red wine and sugar and season well with salt and pepper. Bring to the
boil and then simmer for 20 minutes.

6 Bring a saucepan of lightly salted water to the boil over a medium heat. Add
the gnocchi and cook for 2–3 minutes or until they rise to the top of the pan.
Drain well and transfer to serving dishes. Spoon the sauce over the gnocchi.
Garnish with basil and serve.

These spicy vegetable burgers are delicious, especially in a warm bun or roll and served with the light oven chips.

Vegetable Burgers *and* Chips

1 Cook the spinach in a saucepan of boiling water for 2 minutes. Drain thoroughly and pat dry with kitchen paper. Reserve.

2 Heat 1 tablespoon of the olive oil in a frying pan over a low heat. Add the leek and garlic and sauté for 2–3 minutes. Add the remaining ingredients, except the breadcrumbs, and cook for 5–7 minutes until the vegetables have softened. Toss in the drained spinach and cook for 1 minute.

3 Transfer the mixture to a food processor and process for 30 seconds until almost smooth. Transfer to a bowl, stir in the breadcrumbs, mixing well, and leave until cool enough to handle. Using floured hands, form the mixture into 4 equal-sized burgers. Leave to chill for 30 minutes.

4 To make the chips, cut the potatoes into thin wedges and cook in a saucepan of boiling water for 10 minutes. Drain and toss in the flour and chilli powder. Lay the chips on a baking tray and sprinkle with the olive oil. Cook in a preheated oven, 200°C/400°F/Gas Mark 6, for 30 minutes or until golden.

5 Meanwhile, heat the remaining oil in a frying pan and cook the burgers for 8–10 minutes, turning once. Place each burger in a bun or roll, add some salad, and serve with the chips.

SERVES 4

vegetable burgers
100 g/3½ oz spinach
2 tbsp olive oil
1 leek, chopped
2 garlic cloves, crushed
100 g/3½ oz mushrooms, chopped
300 g/10½ oz firm tofu, drained
    and chopped
1 tsp chilli powder
1 tsp curry powder
1 tbsp chopped fresh coriander
75 g/2¾ oz fresh wholemeal breadcrumbs
burger buns or rolls and salad, to serve

chips
2 large potatoes
2 tbsp plain flour
1 tsp chilli powder
2 tbsp olive oil

NUTRITION
Calories *416*; Sugars *4 g*; Protein *18 g*;
Carbohydrate *64 g*; Fat *17 g*; Saturates *2 g*

⭐⭐⭐   moderate
🖐   45 mins
🕐   1 hr

This pâté is easy to prepare and may be stored in the refrigerator for up to two days. Serve with small toasts, Melba toast or a selection of crudités.

Potato *and* Bean Pâté

SERVES 4

100 g/3½ oz floury potatoes, diced
225 g/8 oz mixed canned beans, such as borlotti, flageolet and kidney beans, drained
1 garlic clove, crushed
2 tsp lime juice
1 tbsp chopped fresh coriander
2 tbsp natural yogurt
salt and pepper
chopped fresh coriander, to garnish

1 Cook the potatoes in a saucepan of boiling water for 10 minutes until tender. Drain well and mash with a fork or potato masher.

2 Transfer the potato to a food processor or blender and add the beans, garlic, lime juice and the fresh coriander. Season to taste with salt and pepper and process for 1 minute until a smooth purée forms. Alternatively, mix the beans with the potato, garlic, lime juice and coriander and mash by hand.

3 Transfer the purée to a bowl and add the yogurt. Mix together thoroughly.

4 Spoon the pâté into a serving dish and garnish with the chopped coriander. Serve immediately or cover with clingfilm and leave to chill before use.

NUTRITION
Calories *84*; Sugars *3 g*; Protein *5 g*;
Carbohydrate *16 g*; Fat *0.5 g*; Saturates *0.1 g*

 easy

 3 mins

 10 mins

🍳 COOK'S TIP

For Melba toast, toast sliced bread lightly on both sides under a preheated high grill and remove the crusts. Holding it flat, slide a sharp knife between the bread to split it horizontally. Cut into triangles and toast the untoasted sides.

These cakes are packed with creamy potato and a variety of mushrooms and will be loved by vegetarians and meat-eaters alike.

Mixed Mushroom Cakes

1 Cook the diced potatoes in a large saucepan of lightly salted boiling water for 10 minutes or until cooked through.

2 Drain the potatoes well, mash with a fork or potato masher and reserve.

3 Meanwhile, melt the butter in a frying pan over a low heat. Add the mushrooms and garlic and cook, stirring constantly, for 5 minutes. Drain.

4 Stir the mushrooms and garlic into the potatoes, together with the beaten egg and snipped chives.

5 Divide the mixture equally into 4 portions and form them into round cakes. Toss them in the flour until the outsides of the cakes are completely coated.

6 Heat the vegetable oil in a frying pan over a medium heat. Add the potato cakes and fry for 10 minutes until golden-brown, turning them over halfway through. Garnish with fresh chives and serve with a crisp salad.

SERVES 4

500 g/1 lb 2 oz floury potatoes, diced
2 tbsp butter
175 g/6 oz mixed mushrooms, chopped
2 garlic cloves, crushed
1 small egg, beaten
1 tbsp snipped fresh chives
25 g/1 oz plain flour, for dusting
3–4 tbsp vegetable oil, for frying
salt and pepper
handful of fresh chives, to garnish
crisp salad, to serve

NUTRITION
Calories *298*; Sugars *0.8 g*; Protein *5 g*; Carbohydrate *22 g*; Fat *22 g*; Saturates *5 g*

 easy

20 mins

25 mins

🖐 **COOK'S TIP**

Prepare the mushroom cakes in advance, cover and leave to chill in the refrigerator for up to 24 hours, if you wish.

These grated potato cakes
are also known as straw
cakes, because they
resemble a straw mat.
Serve them with a tomato
sauce or salad.

Cheese *and* Onion Rösti

SERVES 4

900 g/2 lb potatoes
1 onion, grated
50 g/1¾ oz Gruyère cheese, grated
2 tbsp chopped fresh parsley
1 tbsp olive oil
2 tbsp butter
salt and pepper

to garnish
1 spring onion, shredded
1 small tomato, quartered

1 Parboil the potatoes in a large saucepan of lightly salted boiling water for
10 minutes and leave to cool. Peel the potatoes and grate with a coarse
grater. Place the grated potatoes in a large mixing bowl.

2 Stir in the onion, cheese and parsley. Season well with salt and pepper.
Divide the mixture into 4 portions of equal size and form them into cakes.

3 Heat half of the olive oil and butter in a frying pan over a high heat. Add 2 of
the potato cakes and cook for 1 minute, then reduce the heat and cook for
5 minutes until they are golden underneath. Turn the potato cakes over and
cook for a further 5 minutes.

4 Repeat with the other half of the oil and the remaining butter to cook the
remaining 2 cakes. Transfer the rösti to 4 large, warmed serving plates,
garnish with the spring onion and tomato and serve immediately.

NUTRITION

Calories *307*; Sugars *4 g*; Protein *8 g*;
Carbohydrate *42 g*; Fat *13 g*; Saturates *6 g*

⭐⭐   easy
    10 mins
🕐   40 mins

👨‍🍳 COOK'S TIP

The potato cakes should be flattened as much as possible during cooking,
otherwise the outsides will be cooked before the centres are done.

These fritters make a filling snack. They are an excellent way to use up leftover cooked vegetables.

Potato *and* Cauliflower Fritters

1 Cook the potatoes in a large saucepan of boiling water for 10 minutes until cooked through. Drain well and mash.

2 Meanwhile, cook the cauliflower florets in a separate saucepan of boiling water for 10 minutes. Drain thoroughly.

3 Mix the cauliflower florets into the mashed potato. Stir in the Parmesan cheese and season well with salt and pepper.

4 Separate the whole egg and beat the yolk into the potato and cauliflower.

5 Lightly whisk both the egg whites in a clean bowl, then carefully fold into the potato and cauliflower mixture.

6 Divide the potato and cauliflower mixture equally into 8 portions and then form them into rounds.

7 Heat the vegetable oil in a frying pan over a medium heat. Add the fritters and cook for 3–5 minutes, turning once halfway through cooking.

8 Dust the cooked fritters with a little paprika, if wished, and then serve them immediately accompanied by the crispy chopped bacon.

COOK'S TIP

Any other vegetable, such as broccoli, can be used in this recipe instead of the cauliflower florets, if you prefer.

SERVES 4

225 g/8 oz floury potatoes, diced
225 g/8 oz cauliflower florets
35 g/1¼ oz freshly grated Parmesan cheese
1 egg, plus 1 extra egg white, for coating
3–4 tbsp vegetable oil, for frying
paprika, for dusting (optional)
salt and pepper
crispy bacon rashers, chopped, to serve

NUTRITION
Calories *665*; Sugars *5 g*; Protein *18 g*;
Carbohydrate *98 g*; Fat *25 g*; Saturates *4 g*

  moderate

  10 mins

15–20 mins

Chunks of cooked potato
are coated first in
Parmesan cheese, then
in a light batter before
being fried until golden
for a delicious hot snack.

Fritters *with* Garlic Sauce

SERVES 4

500 g/1 lb 2 oz waxy potatoes, cubed
125 g/4½ oz freshly grated Parmesan cheese
600 ml/1 pint vegetable oil, for deep-frying

sauce
2 tbsp butter
1 onion, halved and sliced
2 garlic cloves, crushed
2½ tbsp plain flour
300 ml/10 fl oz milk
1 tbsp chopped fresh parsley

batter
5 tbsp plain flour
1 small egg
150 ml/5 fl oz milk

NUTRITION
Calories *599*; Sugars *9 g*; Protein *22 g*;
Carbohydrate *42 g*; Fat *39 g*; Saturates *13 g*

easy

20 mins

20–25 mins

1 To make the sauce, melt the butter in a saucepan over a low heat. Add the onion and garlic and cook, stirring frequently, for 2–3 minutes. Add the flour and cook, stirring constantly, for 1 minute.

2 Remove from the heat and stir in the milk and parsley. Return to the heat and bring to the boil. Keep warm.

3 Meanwhile, cook the cubed potatoes in a saucepan of boiling water for 5–10 minutes, until just firm. Do not overcook or they will fall apart.

4 Drain the potatoes and toss them in the Parmesan cheese. If the potatoes are still slightly wet, the cheese will stick to them and coat them well.

5 To make the batter, place the flour in a mixing bowl and gradually beat in the egg and milk until smooth. Dip the potato cubes into the batter to coat them thoroughly.

6 Heat the vegetable oil in a large saucepan or deep-fryer to 180°C/350°F or until a cube of bread browns in 30 seconds. Add the potato fritters and cook for 3–4 minutes or until golden.

7 Remove the fritters with a slotted spoon and drain well. Transfer them to a warmed serving bowl and serve immediately with the garlic sauce.

This quick, chunky omelette has pieces of potato cooked into the egg mixture and is then filled with feta cheese and baby spinach.

Feta *and* Spinach Omelette

1 Heat 25 g/1 oz of the butter in a frying pan over a low heat. Add the potatoes and cook, stirring, for 7–10 minutes until golden. Transfer to a bowl.

2 Add the garlic, paprika and tomatoes to the pan with potatoes and cook for a further 2 minutes.

3 Whisk the eggs together and season with pepper. Pour the eggs into the potatoes and mix well.

4 To make the filling, cook the spinach in a saucepan of boiling water for 1 minute, until just wilted. Drain and refresh under cold running water. Pat dry with kitchen paper. Stir in the fennel seeds, feta cheese and yogurt.

5 Heat one-quarter of the remaining butter in a 15-cm/6-inch omelette pan. Ladle one-quarter of the egg and potato mixture into the pan and cook, turning once, for 2 minutes until set.

6 Spoon one-quarter of the spinach mixture on to one half of the omelette, then fold the omelette in half over the filling. Repeat to make 4 omelettes. Transfer the omelettes to a serving plate.

SERVES 4

75 g/2³/₄ oz butter
1.3 kg/3 lb waxy potatoes, diced
3 garlic cloves, crushed
1 tsp paprika
2 tomatoes, peeled, deseeded and diced
12 eggs
pepper

filling

225 g/8 oz baby spinach
1 tsp fennel seeds
125 g/4¹/₂ oz feta cheese, diced (drained weight)
4 tbsp natural yogurt

NUTRITION

Calories *564*; Sugars *6 g*; Protein *30 g*; Carbohydrate *25 g*; Fat *39 g*; Saturates *19 g*

 easy

 20 mins

25–30 mins

 COOK'S TIP

Use any other cheese, such as blue cheese, instead of the feta, and blanched broccoli instead of the baby spinach, if you prefer.

These oven-baked
mushrooms are covered
with a creamy potato and
mushroom filling topped
with melted cheese.

Creamy Stuffed Mushrooms

SERVES 4

25 g/1 oz dried ceps
225 g/8 oz floury potatoes, diced
25 g/1 oz butter, melted
4 tbsp double cream
2 tbsp chopped fresh chives
8 large open-cap mushrooms
25 g/1 oz Emmenthal cheese, grated
150 ml/5 fl oz vegetable stock
salt and pepper
fresh chives, to garnish
crisp salad, to serve

NUTRITION
Calories 214; Sugars 1 g; Protein 5 g;
Carbohydrate 11 g; Fat 17 g; Saturates 11 g

easy

40 mins

40 mins

1 Place the dried ceps in a small bowl. Add enough boiling water to cover and leave to soak for 20 minutes.

2 Meanwhile, cook the potatoes in a medium saucepan of lightly salted boiling water for 10 minutes until cooked through and tender. Drain the potatoes well and mash until smooth.

3 Drain the ceps and chop them finely. Mix into the mashed potato.

4 Blend the butter, cream and chives together and pour the mixture into the cep and potato mixture, mixing well. Season to taste with salt and pepper.

5 Remove the stalks from the open-cap mushrooms. Chop the stalks and stir them into the potato mixture. Spoon the mixture into the mushrooms and sprinkle the cheese over the top.

6 Arrange the stuffed mushrooms in a shallow ovenproof dish and pour in the vegetable stock. Cover the dish with a lid or foil.

7 Cook in a preheated oven, 220°C/425°F/Gas Mark 7, for 20 minutes. Remove the lid and cook for 5 minutes until golden. Transfer to a serving plate, garnish with a few fresh chives and serve with a crisp salad.

COOK'S TIP

Use fresh mushrooms instead of the dried ceps, if preferred, and stir a mixture of chopped nuts into the mushroom stuffing mixture for extra crunch.

Use any mixture of mushrooms for this creamy layered bake. It can be served straight from the dish in which it is cooked.

Potato *and* Mushroom Bake

1 Grease a shallow round ovenproof dish with the butter.

2 Parboil the potatoes in a saucepan of boiling water for 10 minutes. Drain well. Layer one-quarter of the potatoes in the base of the dish.

3 Arrange one-quarter of the mushrooms on top of the potatoes and sprinkle with one-quarter of the rosemary, chives and garlic. Continue making layers in the same order, finishing with a layer of potatoes on top.

4 Pour the cream over the top of the potatoes, then season to taste with salt and pepper.

5 Cook in a preheated oven, 190°C/375°F/Gas Mark 5, for about 45 minutes or until the bake is golden-brown and piping hot.

6 Garnish with snipped chives and serve immediately straight from the dish.

SERVES 4

25 g/1 oz butter
500 g/1 lb 2 oz waxy potatoes, sliced thinly
150 g/5½ oz sliced mixed mushrooms
1 tbsp chopped fresh rosemary
4 tbsp snipped fresh chives
2 garlic cloves, crushed
150 ml/5 fl oz double cream
salt and pepper
snipped fresh chives, to garnish

NUTRITION
Calories 304; Sugars 2 g; Protein 4 g;
Carbohydrate 20 g; Fat 24 g; Saturates 5 g

 easy

15 mins

55 mins

 COOK'S TIP

For a special occasion, the bake may be made in a lined cake tin and then turned out to serve.

This is a filling Indian sandwich. Spicy potatoes fill the naan breads, which are served with a cool cucumber raita and lime pickle on the side.

Potato-filled Naan Breads

SERVES 4

225 g/8 oz waxy potatoes, scrubbed
   and diced
1 tbsp vegetable oil
1 onion, chopped
2 garlic cloves, crushed
1 tsp ground cumin
1 tsp ground coriander
½ tsp chilli powder
1 tbsp tomato purée
3 tbsp vegetable stock
75 g/2¾ oz baby spinach, shredded
4 small or 2 large naan breads
lime pickle, to serve

raita
150 ml/5 fl oz low-fat natural yogurt
4 tbsp diced cucumber
1 tbsp chopped fresh mint

1 Cook the diced potatoes in a saucepan of boiling water for 10 minutes. Drain thoroughly and reserve.

2 Heat the vegetable oil in a separate saucepan over a medium–low heat. Add the onion and garlic and cook for 3 minutes, stirring. Add the spices and cook for a further 2 minutes.

3 Stir in the potatoes, tomato purée, vegetable stock and spinach. Cook for 5 minutes until the potatoes are tender.

4 Warm the naan breads in a preheated oven, 150°C/300°F/Gas Mark 2, for about 2 minutes.

5 To make the raita, mix the yogurt, cucumber and mint in a small bowl.

6 Remove the naan breads from the oven. Using a sharp knife, cut a pocket in the side of each naan bread. Carefully spoon the spicy potato mixture into each pocket.

7 Serve the filled naan breads immediately with the raita and lime pickle.

NUTRITION
Calories *244*; Sugars *7 g*; Protein *8 g*;
Carbohydrate *37 g*; Fat *8 g*; Saturates *1 g*

easy

10 mins

25 mins

 COOK'S TIP

To give the raita a much stronger flavour, make it in advance and leave to chill in the refrigerator until ready to serve.

These small pasties are made with crisp filo pastry and filled with a tasty spinach and potato mixture flavoured with chilli and tomato.

Potato *and* Spinach Triangles

1 Lightly grease a baking tray with a little butter.

2 Cook the diced potatoes in a large saucepan of lightly salted boiling water for 10 minutes or until cooked through. Drain and place in a mixing bowl.

3 Meanwhile, put the spinach into a saucepan with 2 tablespoons of water, cover and cook over a low heat for 2 minutes, until wilted. Drain the spinach thoroughly, squeezing out excess moisture, and add to the potatoes.

4 Stir in the tomato, chilli powder and lemon juice. Season to taste with salt and pepper.

5 Lightly brush 8 sheets of filo pastry with a little melted butter. Spread out 4 of the sheets and lay the other 4 on top of each. Cut them into rectangles measuring about 20 x 10 cm/8 x 4 inches.

6 Spoon the potato and spinach mixture on to one end of each rectangle. Fold a corner of the pastry over the filling, fold the pointed end back over the pastry strip, then fold over the remaining pastry to form a triangle.

7 Place the triangles on the baking tray and bake in a preheated oven, 190°C/375°F/Gas Mark 5, for 20 minutes or until golden-brown.

8 To make the lemon mayonnaise, mix the mayonnaise, lemon juice and lemon rind together in a small bowl. Serve the potato and spinach triangles warm or cold with the lemon mayonnaise.

SERVES 4

25 g/1 oz butter, melted, plus extra for greasing
225 g/8 oz waxy potatoes, diced finely
500 g/1 lb 2 oz baby spinach
1 tomato, deseeded and chopped
¼ tsp chilli powder
½ tsp lemon juice
225 g/8 oz (8 sheets) filo pastry, thawed if frozen
salt and pepper

lemon mayonnaise
150 ml/5 fl oz mayonnaise
2 tsp lemon juice
grated rind of 1 lemon

NUTRITION
Calories *514*; Sugars *4 g*; Protein *9 g*; Carbohydrate *37 g*; Fat *37 g*; Saturates *8 g*

✪✪✪   moderate

◔   25 mins

🕐   35 mins

This makes a luscious side dish to serve with meat, or serve it on its own as a satisfying vegetarian main course. Goat's cheese is a traditional food of Mexico.

Potatoes *with* Goat's Cheese

SERVES 4

1.25 kg/2 lb 12 oz baking potatoes, cut into chunks
pinch of salt
pinch of sugar
200 ml/7 fl oz crème fraîche
125 ml/4 fl oz vegetable or chicken stock
3 garlic cloves, chopped finely
a few shakes of bottled chipotle salsa, or 1 dried chipotle, reconstituted, deseeded and thinly sliced
225 g/8 oz goat's cheese, sliced
175 g/6 oz mozzarella or Cheddar cheese, grated
50 g/1¾ oz Parmesan or pecorino cheese, grated

1 Put the potatoes into a saucepan of water with the salt and sugar. Bring to the boil and cook for about 10 minutes until they are half cooked.

2 Combine the crème fraîche with the stock, garlic and chipotle salsa.

3 Arrange half the potatoes in a casserole. Pour half the crème fraîche sauce over the potatoes and cover with the goat's cheese. Top with the remaining potatoes and the sauce.

4 Sprinkle with the grated mozzarella or Cheddar cheese, then with either the grated Parmesan or pecorino cheese.

5 Bake in a preheated oven, 180°C/350°F/Gas Mark 4, for about 25 minutes until the potatoes are tender and the cheese topping is lightly golden and has become crisp in places. Serve immediately.

NUTRITION
Calories *725*; Sugars *4 g*; Protein *30 g*;
Carbohydrate *56 g*; Fat *43 g*; Saturates *28 g*

easy

2 mins

35 mins

This fish pâté is given a tart fruity flavour by the cooked gooseberries, which complement the fish perfectly.

Smoked Fish *and* Potato Pâté

1 Cook the diced potatoes in a saucepan of boiling water for 10 minutes until tender, then drain well.

2 Place the cooked potatoes in a food processor or blender.

3 Add the skinned and flaked smoked mackerel and process for 30 seconds until fairly smooth. Alternatively, place the ingredients in a bowl and then mash them by hand with a fork.

4 Add the cooked gooseberries, lemon juice and crème fraîche to the fish and potato mixture. Blend for a further 10 seconds or mash well.

5 Stir in the capers, gherkin, dill pickle, and fresh dill. Season to taste with salt and pepper.

6 Transfer the fish pâté to a serving dish, garnish with lemon wedges and serve with slices of toast or warm crusty bread, cut into chunks or slices.

SERVES 4

650 g/1 lb 7 oz floury potatoes, diced
300 g/10½ oz smoked mackerel, skinned and flaked
75 g/2¾ oz cooked gooseberries
2 tsp lemon juice
2 tbsp low-fat crème fraîche
1 tbsp capers
1 gherkin, chopped
1 tbsp chopped dill pickle
1 tbsp chopped fresh dill
salt and pepper
lemon wedges, to garnish
toast or warm crusty bread, to serve

NUTRITION
Calories *418*; Sugars *4 g*; Protein *18 g*; Carbohydrate *32 g*; Fat *25 g*; Saturates *6 g*

⭐⭐ easy
🕐 20 mins
🕐 10 mins

 COOK'S TIP

Use stewed, canned or bottled cooked gooseberries for convenience and to save time, or when fresh gooseberries are out of season.

These fish cakes make a satisfying and quick mid-week supper. The tomato sauce is flavoured with a tempting combination of lemon, garlic and basil.

Tuna Fish Cakes

SERVES 4

225 g/8 oz potatoes, cubed
1 tbsp olive oil
1 large shallot, chopped finely
1 garlic clove, chopped finely
1 tsp thyme leaves
400 g/14 oz canned tuna in olive oil, drained
grated rind of ½ lemon
1 tbsp chopped fresh parsley
2–3 tbsp plain flour
1 egg, beaten lightly
115 g/4 oz fresh breadcrumbs
125 ml/4 fl oz vegetable oil, for shallow-frying
salt and pepper
mixed salad, to serve

quick tomato sauce
2 tbsp olive oil
400 g/14 oz canned chopped tomatoes
1 garlic clove, crushed
½ tsp sugar
grated rind of ½ lemon
1 tbsp chopped fresh basil

NUTRITION

Calories *638*; Sugars *5 g*; Protein *35 g*;
Carbohydrate *38 g*; Fat *40 g*; Saturates *5 g*

★★★   moderate

🕐   5 mins

🕐   1 hr 10 mins

1 To make the tuna fish cakes, cook the potatoes in plenty of salted boiling water for 12–15 minutes until tender. Mash, leaving a few lumps, and reserve.

2 Heat the oil in a frying pan over a low heat. Add the shallot and cook gently for 5 minutes until softened. Add the garlic and thyme leaves and cook for a further 1 minute. Leave to cool slightly, then add to the potatoes with the tuna, lemon rind, parsley and seasoning. Mix well, but leave some texture.

3 Form the mixture into 6–8 cakes. Dip the cakes first in the flour, then the egg and finally the breadcrumbs to coat. Leave to chill for 30 minutes.

4 To make the tomato sauce, put the olive oil, tomatoes, garlic, sugar, lemon rind, basil and salt and pepper to taste into a saucepan and bring to the boil. Cover and simmer for 30 minutes. Uncover and simmer for 15 minutes until thickened.

5 Heat enough vegetable oil in a frying pan to cover the base generously. Add the fish cakes, in batches, and fry for 3–4 minutes on each side until golden and crisp. Drain on kitchen paper while you fry the remaining fish cakes. Serve the tuna fish cakes hot with the tomato sauce and a mixed salad.

🍳 **COOK'S TIP**

The tuna can be replaced by cooked, flaked salmon or haddock, if preferred. Omit the thyme leaves.

As well as being a simple supper dish, this would make a delicious addition to a brunch menu.

Salt Cod Hash

1 Sprinkle the salt over both sides of the cod fillet. Place in a shallow dish, cover and leave to chill in the refrigerator for 48 hours. When ready to cook, remove the cod from the refrigerator and rinse under cold running water. Leave to soak in cold water for 2 hours, then drain well.

2 Bring a large saucepan of water to the boil over a low heat. Add the fish then remove from the heat and leave to stand for 10 minutes. Drain the fish on kitchen paper and flake the flesh. Reserve. Discard the soaking water.

3 Bring a saucepan of water to the boil over a medium heat. Add the eggs and simmer for 7–9 minutes from when the water returns to the boil – 7 minutes for a slightly soft centre, 9 for a firm centre. Drain, then plunge the eggs into cold water. Shell the eggs and roughly chop. Reserve.

4 Heat the olive oil in a large frying pan over a medium heat. Add the bacon and cook for 4–5 minutes until crisp and browned. Remove with a slotted spoon and drain on kitchen paper. Put the potatoes and garlic into the pan and cook over a medium heat for 8–10 minutes until crisp and golden. Meanwhile, toast the bread on both sides. Drizzle the bread with olive oil and reserve.

5 Add the tomatoes, bacon, fish, vinegar and chopped egg to the potatoes and garlic. Cook for 2 minutes. Stir in the parsley and season to taste with salt and pepper. Put the toast on to serving plates, top with the hash and garnish with a few sprigs of fresh parsley. Serve.

SERVES 4

25 g/1 oz sea salt
750 g/1 lb 10 oz fresh boneless cod fillet
4 eggs
3 tbsp olive oil, plus extra for drizzling
8 rindless smoked streaky bacon
  rashers, chopped
700 g/1 lb 9 oz old potatoes, diced
8 garlic cloves
8 thick slices good-quality white bread
2 plum tomatoes, peeled and chopped
2 tsp red wine vinegar
2 tbsp chopped fresh parsley
salt and pepper
fresh flat-leaved parsley sprigs, to garnish

NUTRITION

Calories *857*; Sugars *5 g*; Protein *58 g*;
Carbohydrate *82 g*; Fat *36 g*; Saturates *10 g*

 challenging

50 hrs 5 mins

30 mins

These small crab cakes are based on a traditional Thai recipe. They make a delicious snack when served with this sweet and sour cucumber sauce.

Thai Potato Crab Cakes

S E R V E S 4

450 g/1 lb floury potatoes, diced
175 g/6 oz white crab meat, drained if canned
4 spring onions, chopped
1 tsp light soy sauce
½ tsp sesame oil
1 tsp chopped lemon grass
1 tsp lime juice
3 tbsp plain flour
2 tbsp vegetable oil
salt and pepper

sauce
4 tbsp finely chopped cucumber
2 tbsp clear honey
1 tbsp garlic wine vinegar
½ tsp light soy sauce
1 chopped fresh red chilli

to garnish
1 fresh red chilli, sliced
cucumber slices

N U T R I T I O N
Calories *254*; Sugars *9 g*; Protein *12 g*;
Carbohydrate *40 g*; Fat *6 g*; Saturates *1 g*

 easy
 10 mins
 30 mins

1 Cook the diced potatoes in a saucepan of boiling water for 10 minutes until cooked through. Drain well and mash.

2 Mix the crab meat into the cooked potatoes with the spring onions, soy sauce, sesame oil, lemon grass, lime juice and flour. Season to taste with salt and pepper.

3 Using floured hands, divide the potato mixture equally into 8 portions and form them into small rounds.

4 Heat the vegetable oil in a preheated wok or frying pan over a medium heat. Add the cakes, 4 at a time and cook for 5–7 minutes, turning once. Keep warm and repeat with the remaining crab cakes.

5 Meanwhile, make the sauce. Mix the cucumber, honey, vinegar, soy sauce and red chilli in a small serving bowl.

6 Transfer the crab cakes to a large serving plate and garnish with the sliced red chilli and cucumber slices. Serve with the sauce.

These crisp little vegetable and prawn cakes make an ideal light lunch or supper, accompanied by a salad.

Prawn Rösti

1 To make the salsa, mix the tomatoes, mango, chilli, onion, coriander, chives, olive oil, lemon juice and seasoning. Leave to stand to let the flavours infuse.

2 Using a food processor or the fine blade of a box grater, finely grate the potatoes, celeriac, carrot and onion. Mix together with the prawns, flour and egg. Season well with salt and pepper and reserve.

3 Divide the prawn mixture equally into 8 equal portions. Press each into a greased 10-cm/4-inch biscuit cutter (if you only have 1 cutter, you can simply shape the rösti individually).

4 Heat a shallow layer of oil in a large frying pan over a medium heat. When hot, transfer the vegetable cakes, still in the cutters, to the frying pan, in 4 batches, if necessary. When the oil sizzles underneath, remove the cutters. Fry gently, pressing down with a spatula, for 6–8 minutes on each side, until crisp and browned and the vegetables are tender. Drain on kitchen paper and keep warm in a preheated oven. Serve hot with the tomato salsa and a mixed salad.

SERVES 4

350 g/12 oz potatoes
350 g/12 oz celeriac
1 carrot
½ small onion
225 g/8 oz cooked peeled prawns, thawed if frozen and well-drained on kitchen paper
2½ tbsp plain flour
1 egg, beaten lightly
3–4 tbsp vegetable oil, for frying
salt and pepper
mixed salad, to serve

cherry tomato salsa
225 g/8 oz mixed cherry tomatoes such as baby plum, yellow and orange, quartered
½ small mango, diced finely
1 fresh red chilli, deseeded and chopped
½ small red onion, chopped finely
1 tbsp chopped fresh coriander
1 tbsp snipped fresh chives
2 tbsp olive oil
2 tsp lemon juice

NUTRITION
Calories *445*; Sugars *9 g*; Protein *19 g*; Carbohydrate *29 g*; Fat *29 g*; Saturates *4 g*

⭐⭐⭐ moderate

🖐 10 mins

🕐 1 hr

You need to use floury-textured old potatoes to make these tasty fritters. Any white fish of your choice may be used.

Spicy Fish *and* Potato Fritters

SERVES 4

500 g/1 lb 2 oz potatoes, peeled and cut into even-sized pieces
500 g/1 lb 2 oz white fish fillets, such as cod or haddock, skinned and boned
6 spring onions, sliced
1 fresh green chilli, deseeded
2 garlic cloves, peeled
1 tsp salt
1 tbsp medium or hot curry paste
2 eggs, beaten
150 g/5½ oz fresh white breadcrumbs
125 ml/4 fl oz vegetable oil, for shallow-frying
mango chutney, to serve (optional)

to garnish
fresh coriander sprigs
lime wedges

1 Cook the potatoes in a saucepan of lightly salted boiling water until tender. Drain well, return the potatoes to the pan and place over a medium heat for a few moments to dry off. Leave to cool slightly, then place in a food processor with the fish, onions, chilli, garlic, salt and curry paste. Process until the ingredients are very finely chopped and blended.

2 Transfer the potato mixture to a bowl and mix in 2 tablespoons of beaten egg and 55 g/2 oz of the breadcrumbs. Place the remaining beaten egg and breadcrumbs in separate dishes.

3 Divide the potato mixture equally into 8 portions and, using a spoon to help you (the mixture is quite soft), dip each potato portion first in the beaten egg and then coat it in the breadcrumbs. When each portion is evenly coated, carefully shape it into an oval.

4 Heat enough vegetable oil for shallow-frying in a large frying pan over a medium heat. When hot, fry the fritters for 3–4 minutes, turning frequently, until golden-brown and cooked through.

5 Drain on kitchen paper and garnish with a few sprigs of fresh coriander and lime wedges. Serve the fritters hot with mango chutney, if wished.

NUTRITION
Calories *349*; Sugars *4 g*; Protein *31 g*; Carbohydrate *41 g*; Fat *8 g*; Saturates *1 g*

 moderate

15 mins

25 mins

These fritters are delicious served with salad leaves, a fresh vegetable salsa or a chilli sauce dip.

Chicken *and* Herb Fritters

1 Blend the mashed potatoes, chicken, ham, mixed herbs and 1 egg in a large bowl, and season well with salt and pepper.

2 Form the mixture into small balls or flat pancakes.

3 Add a little milk to the second egg and mix together.

4 Place the breadcrumbs on a plate. Dip the balls in the egg and milk mixture, then roll in the breadcrumbs to coat them completely.

5 Heat the vegetable oil in a large frying pan over a medium heat. Add the fritters and fry until golden-brown. Garnish the fritters with a few sprigs of fresh parsley and serve immediately with a crisp mixed salad.

SERVES 4

500 g/1 lb 2 oz mashed potatoes, with butter added
225 g/8 oz chopped cooked chicken
115 g/4 oz cooked ham, chopped finely
1 tbsp mixed herbs
2 eggs, beaten lightly
milk
fresh brown breadcrumbs, for coating
125 ml/4 fl oz vegetable oil, for shallow-frying
salt and pepper
fresh parsley sprigs, to garnish
crisp mixed salad, to serve

NUTRITION

Calories 33; Sugars 1 g; Protein 16 g; Carbohydrate 17 g; Fat 23 g; Saturates 5 g

 COOK'S TIP

A mixture of chopped fresh tarragon and parsley makes a flavoursome addition to these tasty fritters.

moderate

5 mins

10–15 mins

These meatballs are delicious served with warm crusty bread to mop up the spicy sauce.

Meatballs *in* Spicy Sauce

SERVES 4

225 g/8 oz floury potatoes, diced
225 g/8 oz minced beef or lamb
1 onion, chopped finely
1 tbsp chopped fresh coriander
1 celery stick, chopped finely
2 garlic cloves, crushed
25 g/1 oz butter
1 tbsp vegetable oil
salt and pepper
chopped fresh coriander, to garnish

sauce

1 tbsp vegetable oil
1 onion, chopped finely
2 tsp soft brown sugar
400 g/14 oz canned chopped tomatoes
1 fresh green chilli, chopped
1 tsp paprika
150 ml/5 fl oz vegetable stock
2 tsp cornflour

NUTRITION

Calories 95; Sugars 2.7 g; Protein 4.5 g;
Carbohydrate 6.6 g; Fat 5.8 g; Saturates 2.3 g

⭐⭐ easy

🕐 5 mins

🕐 1 hr 10 mins

1 Cook the diced potatoes in a saucepan of boiling water for 25 minutes, until cooked through. Drain and transfer to a mixing bowl. Mash until smooth.

2 Add the minced beef or lamb, onion, coriander, celery and garlic to the mashed potatoes and mix together well.

3 Bring the mixture together with your hands and roll it into 20 small balls.

4 To make the sauce, heat the vegetable oil in a saucepan over a low heat. Add the onion and sauté for 5 minutes. Add the remaining sauce ingredients and bring to the boil, stirring. Reduce the heat and simmer for 20 minutes.

5 Meanwhile, heat the butter and vegetable oil for the meatballs in a frying pan over a medium heat. Add the meatballs, in batches, and cook for about 10–15 minutes until browned, turning frequently. Keep warm while cooking the remainder. Serve the meatballs in a warmed, shallow ovenproof dish with the sauce poured around them and garnished with the fresh coriander.

 COOK'S TIP

Make the meatballs in advance and chill or freeze them for later use. Make sure you thaw them thoroughly before cooking.

This classic potato dish may be served plain as an accompaniment or with added ingredients and a cheese sauce as a snack.

Croquettes *with* Ham

1 Place the potatoes in a saucepan with the milk and bring to the boil. Reduce to a simmer until the liquid has been absorbed and the potatoes are cooked.

2 Add the butter and mash the potatoes. Stir in the spring onions, Cheddar cheese, ham, celery, egg and flour. Season to taste with salt and pepper and leave to cool.

3 To make the coating for the croquettes, whisk the eggs in a bowl. Put the breadcrumbs in a separate bowl.

4 Form the potato mixture into 8 balls. First dip them in the egg, then in the breadcrumbs. Reserve.

5 To make the sauce, melt the butter in a small pan over a low heat. Add the flour and cook for 1 minute. Remove from the heat and stir in the milk, stock, cheese, mustard and coriander. Bring to the boil, stirring until thickened. Reduce the heat and keep warm, stirring occasionally.

6 Heat the vegetable oil in a deep-fryer to 180°–190°C/350°–375°F and fry the croquettes, in batches, for 5 minutes until golden. Drain well and serve with the sauce.

SERVES 4

450 g/1 lb floury potatoes, diced
300 ml/10 fl oz milk
2 tbsp butter
4 spring onions, chopped
75 g/2¾ oz Cheddar cheese, grated
50 g/1¾ oz smoked ham, chopped
1 celery stick, diced
1 egg, beaten
5 tbsp plain flour
600 ml/1 pint vegetable oil, for deep-frying
salt and pepper

coating
2 eggs, beaten
125 g/4½ oz fresh wholemeal breadcrumbs

sauce
2 tbsp butter
2 tbsp plain flour
150 ml/5 fl oz milk
150 ml/5 fl oz vegetable stock
75 g/2¾ oz Cheddar cheese, grated
1 tsp Dijon mustard
1 tbsp chopped fresh coriander

NUTRITION
Calories *792*; Sugars *8 g*; Protein *28 g*;
Carbohydrate *53 g*; Fat *54 g*; Saturates *21 g*

★★★ moderate
 5 mins
 30 mins

This is an old Irish recipe, usually served with a piece of bacon, but it is equally delicious with a vegetarian main course dish.

Colcannon

SERVES 4

225 g/8 oz green cabbage, shredded
5 tbsp milk
225 g/8 oz floury potatoes, diced
1 large leek, chopped
pinch of freshly grated nutmeg
15 g/½ oz butter, melted
salt and pepper

1 Cook the shredded cabbage in a large saucepan of boiling salted water for 7–10 minutes. Drain thoroughly and reserve.

2 Meanwhile, bring the milk to the boil in a separate saucepan over a low heat. Add the potatoes and leek, then reduce the heat and simmer for about 15–20 minutes or until the potatoes and leek are cooked through.

3 Stir in the nutmeg and mash the potatoes and leek together.

4 Add the cabbage to the mashed potato and leek mixture. Mix together thoroughly until well blended. Season to taste with salt and pepper.

5 Spoon the mixture into a large warmed serving dish, making a hollow in the centre with the back of a spoon.

6 Pour the melted butter into the hollow and serve immediately.

NUTRITION

Calories 102; Sugars 4 g; Protein 4 g; Carbohydrate 14 g; Fat 4 g; Saturates 2 g

easy

20 mins

20 mins

 COOK'S TIP

There are many different varieties of cabbage, which produce hearts at varying times of year, so you can be sure of being able to make this delicious cabbage and potato dish all year round.

Classic fried potatoes are given extra flavour by pre-cooking the potatoes and shallow-frying them in butter with onion, garlic and herbs.

Fried Potatoes *with* Onions

1 Cook the cubed potatoes in a saucepan of boiling water for 10 minutes. Drain the potatoes thoroughly.

2 Melt the butter in a large, heavy-based frying pan over a low heat. Add the onion wedges, garlic and lemon juice and cook for 2-3 minutes, stirring.

3 Add the potatoes to the pan and mix well to coat in the butter mixture.

4 Reduce the heat, cover the frying pan and cook for 25–30 minutes or until the potatoes are golden and tender.

5 Sprinkle the chopped thyme over the top of the potatoes and season to taste with salt and pepper.

6 Garnish with a few sprigs of fresh thyme, if wished, then serve immediately as a side dish to accompany grilled meats or fish.

SERVES 4

900 g/2 lb waxy potatoes, cubed
125 g/4$\frac{1}{2}$ oz butter
1 red onion, cut into 8 wedges
2 garlic cloves, crushed
1 tsp lemon juice
2 tbsp chopped fresh thyme
salt and pepper
fresh thyme sprigs, to garnish (optional)

NUTRITION
Calories *140*; Sugars *1.2 g*; Protein *1.8 g*;
Carbohydrate *14 g*; Fat *8.8 g*; Saturates *5.7 g*

 very easy

 5 mins

🕐 40 mins

🍳 **COOK'S TIP**

The beautifully coloured purple-red onions used here have a mild, slightly sweet flavour as well as looking extremely attractive. Because of their mild taste, they are equally good eaten raw in salads.

In Indian cooking there are many variations of spicy potatoes. In this recipe, spinach is added for both colour and flavour.

Spicy Indian Potatoes

SERVES 4

½ tsp coriander seeds
1 tsp cumin seeds
4 tbsp vegetable oil
2 cardamon pods
1 tsp grated fresh root ginger
1 fresh red chilli, chopped
1 onion, chopped
2 garlic cloves, crushed
450 g/1 lb new potatoes, quartered
150 ml/5 fl oz vegetable stock
675 g/1 lb 8 oz fresh spinach, chopped
4 tbsp natural yogurt
salt and pepper

1 Grind the coriander and cumin seeds, using a pestle and mortar.

2 Heat the vegetable oil in a frying pan over a medium-low heat. Add the ground coriander and cumin seeds, with the cardamom pods and ginger and cook for about 2 minutes.

3 Add the chopped chilli, onion and garlic to the frying pan. Cook for a further 2 minutes, stirring frequently.

4 Add the potatoes to the pan together with the vegetable stock. Cook gently for 30 minutes or until the potatoes are cooked through.

5 Add the spinach to the pan and cook for a further 5 minutes.

6 Remove the pan from the heat and stir in the yogurt. Season to taste with salt and pepper. Transfer to a serving dish and serve.

NUTRITION

Calories 65; Sugars 1.9 g; Protein 2.5 g;
Carbohydrate 6.5 g; Fat 3.4 g; Saturates 0.4 g

⭐⭐   easy
🕐   10 mins
🕐   40 mins

 COOK'S TIP

Use frozen spinach instead of fresh spinach, if you prefer. Thaw and drain it thoroughly before adding it to the dish, otherwise it will turn soggy.

This is a rich recipe that is best served with plain dark meats, such as beef or game, to complement the flavour.

Potatoes *in* Red Wine

1 Melt the butter in a heavy-based frying pan over a medium heat. Add the potatoes and cook gently for 5 minutes, stirring constantly.

2 Add the red wine, beef stock and shallots. Season to taste with salt and pepper and simmer for 30 minutes.

3 Stir in the mushrooms and chopped herbs and cook for 5 minutes.

4 Transfer the potatoes and mushrooms to a warmed serving dish. Garnish with fresh sage leaves or coriander sprigs and serve immediately.

SERVES 4

125 g/4½ oz butter
450 g/1 lb new potatoes, halved
200 ml/7 fl oz red wine
6 tbsp beef stock
8 shallots, halved
125 g/4½ oz oyster mushrooms
1 tbsp chopped fresh sage or coriander
salt and pepper
sage leaves or fresh coriander sprigs, to garnish

NUTRITION
Calories *116*; Sugars *1.4 g*; Protein *1.5 g*;
Carbohydrate *7 g*; Fat *8.7 g*; Saturates *5.7 g*

✪✪✪   moderate
       5 mins
       45 mins

 COOK'S TIP

If oyster mushrooms are unavailable, other mushrooms, such as large open-cap mushrooms, can be used instead.

This simple spicy dish is
ideal with a plain main
course. The nuts and celery
add extra crunch.

Gingered Potatoes

SERVES 4

675 g/1 lb 8 oz waxy potatoes, cubed
2 tbsp vegetable oil
4 tsp grated fresh root ginger
1 fresh red chilli, chopped
1 celery stick, chopped
25 g/1 oz cashew nuts
few strands of saffron
3 tbsp boiling water
70 g/2½ oz butter
celery leaves, to garnish

1 Cook the potatoes in a saucepan of boiling water for 10 minutes, then drain.

2 Heat the vegetable oil in a heavy-based frying pan over a medium heat. Add the potatoes and cook, stirring constantly, for about 3–4 minutes.

3 Add the ginger, chilli, celery and cashew nuts and cook for a further 1 minute.

4 Meanwhile, place the saffron strands in a small bowl. Add the boiling water and leave to soak for 5 minutes.

5 Add the butter to the pan, reduce the heat and stir in the saffron mixture. Cook over a low heat for 10 minutes or until the potatoes are tender.

6 Transfer to a large, warmed serving dish, garnish with the celery leaves and serve immediately.

NUTRITION

Calories 325; Sugars 1 g; Protein 5 g;
Carbohydrate 30 g; Fat 21 g; Saturates 9 g

easy

20 mins

30 mins

 COOK'S TIP

Use a non-stick, heavy-based frying pan because the potato mixture is fairly dry and may stick to an ordinary pan.

In this sweet and sour dish, tender vegetables are simply stir-fried with spices and coconut milk, and flavoured with lime.

Potato Stir-fry

1 Using a sharp knife, cut the potatoes into small cubes.

2 Cook the diced potatoes in a large saucepan of boiling water for 5 minutes. Drain thoroughly.

3 Heat the vegetable oil in a preheated wok or large frying pan, swirling the oil around the base of the wok until it is really hot.

4 Add the potatoes, peppers, carrot, courgette, garlic and chilli to the wok and stir-fry the vegetables for 2–3 minutes.

5 Stir in the spring onions, coconut milk, lemon grass and lime juice and stir-fry the mixture for a further 5 minutes.

6 Add the lime rind and chopped fresh coriander and stir-fry for 1 minute. Serve immediately while hot.

SERVES 4

900 g/2 lb waxy potatoes
2 tbsp vegetable oil
1 yellow pepper, diced
1 red pepper, diced
1 carrot, cut into matchsticks
1 courgette, cut into matchsticks
2 garlic cloves, crushed
1 fresh red chilli, sliced
1 bunch of spring onions, halved lengthways
125 ml/4 fl oz coconut milk
1 tsp chopped lemon grass
2 tsp lime juice
finely grated rind of 1 lime
1 tbsp chopped fresh coriander

NUTRITION
Calories *138*; Sugars *5 g*; Protein *2 g*;
Carbohydrate *20 g*; Fat *6 g*; Saturates *1 g*

⭐⭐   easy
🕐   10 mins
🕐   20 mins

 COOK'S TIP

Make sure the potatoes are not overcooked at Step 2, otherwise the potato pieces will disintegrate when they are stir-fried in the wok.

This recipe takes a while to prepare, but it is well worth the effort. The golden potato slices coated in breadcrumbs and cheese are delicious.

Cheese *and* Potato Slices

SERVES 4

900 g/2 lb waxy potatoes, unpeeled and sliced thickly
70 g/2½ oz fresh white breadcrumbs
40 g/1½ oz freshly grated Parmesan cheese
1½ tsp chilli powder
2 eggs, beaten
600 ml/1 pint vegetable oil, for deep-frying
chilli powder, for dusting (optional)

1 Cook the potatoes in a saucepan of boiling water for about 10–15 minutes or until the potatoes are just tender. Drain thoroughly.

2 Mix the breadcrumbs, cheese and chilli powder in a bowl, then transfer to a shallow dish. Pour the beaten eggs into a separate shallow dish.

3 Dip the potato slices first in the egg and then roll them in the breadcrumb mixture to coat completely.

4 Heat the vegetable oil in a large saucepan or deep-fryer to 180°C/350°F, or until a cube of bread browns in 30 seconds. Add the cheese and potato slices, in several batches, and cook for 4–5 minutes or until golden-brown.

5 Remove the cooked cheese and potato slices with a slotted spoon and drain thoroughly on kitchen paper. Keep the cheese and potato slices warm while you cook the remaining batches.

6 Transfer the cheese and potato slices to 4 warmed serving plates. Dust lightly with chilli powder (if using) and serve immediately.

NUTRITION
Calories *560*; Sugars *3 g*; Protein *19 g*;
Carbohydrate *55 g*; Fat *31 g*; Saturates *7 g*

 easy

 10 mins

🕐 40 mins

🍳 **COOK'S TIP**

The cheese and potato slices may be coated in the breadcrumb mixture in advance and then stored in the refrigerator until ready to use.

This dish is ideal with grilled or barbecued foods, because the potatoes themselves may be cooked by either method.

Grilled Potatoes *with* Lime

1 Cut the potatoes into 1-cm/½-inch slices.

2 Cook the potatoes in a saucepan of boiling water for 5–7 minutes – they should still be quite firm. Remove the potatoes with a slotted spoon and drain them thoroughly.

3 Line a grill pan with foil. Place the potato slices on top of the foil.

4 Brush the potatoes with the melted butter and sprinkle the thyme on top. Season to taste with salt and pepper.

5 Cook the potatoes under a preheated medium–hot grill for 10 minutes, turning once during cooking.

6 Meanwhile, make the lime mayonnaise. Mix the mayonnaise, lime juice, lime rind, garlic and paprika together in a small bowl. Season to taste with salt and pepper

7 Dust the potato slices with paprika and serve with the lime mayonnaise.

SERVES 4

450 g/1 lb potatoes, unpeeled and scrubbed
40 g/1½ oz butter, melted
2 tbsp chopped fresh thyme
paprika, for dusting
salt and pepper

lime mayonnaise
150 ml/5 fl oz mayonnaise
2 tsp lime juice
finely grated rind of 1 lime
1 garlic clove, crushed
pinch of paprika

NUTRITION
Calories *253*; Sugars *0.7 g*; Protein *1.8 g*;
Carbohydrate *12 g*; Fat *22 g*; Saturates *5.8 g*

easy

10 mins

15–20 mins

🧑‍🍳 COOK'S TIP

For an impressive side dish, thread the potato slices on to skewers and cook over medium–hot barbecue coals.

These home-made chips are flavoured with spices and cooked in the oven. Serve with Lime Mayonnaise (see page 91).

Spicy Potato Fries

SERVES 4

4 large waxy potatoes
2 sweet potatoes
4 tbsp butter, melted
½ tsp chilli powder
1 tsp garam masala
salt

1 Cut the potatoes and sweet potatoes into slices about 1-cm/½-inch thick, then cut them into chip shapes.

2 Place the potatoes in a large bowl of cold salted water. Leave the potatoes to soak for 20 minutes.

3 Remove the potato slices with a slotted spoon and drain thoroughly. Pat with kitchen paper until they are completely dry.

4 Pour the melted butter on to a baking tray. Transfer the potato slices to the baking tray and spread out evenly.

5 Sprinkle with the chilli powder and garam masala, turning the potato slices to coat them with the mixture.

6 Cook the chips in a preheated oven, 200°C/400°F/Gas Mark 6, for about 40 minutes, turning frequently, until browned and cooked through.

7 Drain the chips on kitchen paper to remove the excess oil and serve.

NUTRITION
Calories 328; Sugars 2 g; Protein 5 g;
Carbohydrate 56 g; Fat 11 g; Saturates 7 g

✪✪　　easy
🕐　　35 mins
🕐　　40 mins

  COOK'S TIP

Rinsing the potatoes in cold water before cooking removes the starch, thus preventing them from sticking together. Soaking the potatoes in a bowl of cold salted water actually makes the cooked chips crisper.

Small new potatoes are scrubbed and boiled in their skins, before being coated in a chilli mixture and roasted to perfection in the oven.

Chilli Roast Potatoes

1 Cook the potatoes in a saucepan of boiling water for 10 minutes, then drain.

2 Pour a little of the vegetable oil into a shallow roasting tin to coat the base. Heat the oil in a preheated oven, 200°C/400°F/Gas Mark 6, for 10 minutes. Add the potatoes to the tin and brush them with the hot oil.

3 Mix the chilli powder, caraway seeds and salt together in a small bowl. Sprinkle the mixture over the potatoes, turning to coat them all over.

4 Add the remaining oil to the tin and roast in the oven for about 15 minutes or until the potatoes are cooked through.

5 Using a slotted spoon, remove the potatoes from the the oil, draining them well, and transfer them to a large, warmed serving dish. Sprinkle the chopped basil over the top and serve immediately.

SERVES 4

500 g/1 lb 2 oz small new potatoes, scrubbed
150 ml/5 fl oz vegetable oil
1 tsp chilli powder
½ tsp caraway seeds
1 tsp salt
1 tbsp chopped fresh basil

NUTRITION

Calories *178*; Sugars *2 g*; Protein *2 g*;
Carbohydrate *18 g*; Fat *11 g*; Saturates *1 g*

⭐⭐   easy
🍳   5–10 mins
🕐   30 mins

 COOK'S TIP

Use any other spice of your choice with these roast potatoes, such as curry powder or paprika, for a variation in flavour.

This is a very simple way to jazz up roast potatoes. Serve them in the same way as plain roast potatoes, with roasted meats or fish.

Parmesan Potatoes

SERVES 4

1.3 kg/3 lb potatoes
50 g/1¾ oz freshly grated Parmesan cheese
pinch of freshly grated nutmeg
1 tbsp chopped fresh parsley
4 smoked bacon rashers, cut into strips
125 ml/4 fl oz vegetable oil, for roasting
salt

1 Cut the potatoes in half lengthways and cook them in a saucepan of boiling salted water for 10 minutes. Drain thoroughly.

2 Mix the Parmesan cheese, nutmeg and parsley together in a shallow bowl.

3 Roll the potato pieces in the cheese mixture to coat them completely. Shake off any excess. Reserve.

4 Pour a little vegetable oil into a roasting tin and heat in a preheated oven, 200°C/400°F/Gas Mark 6, for 10 minutes. Remove from the oven and add the potatoes to the tin. Return the potatoes to the oven and cook for 30 minutes, turning once.

5 Remove the potatoes from the oven and sprinkle the bacon on top of the potatoes. Return to the oven for 15 minutes or until the potatoes and bacon are cooked. Drain off any excess fat and serve.

NUTRITION
Calories 307; Sugars 2 g; Protein 11 g;
Carbohydrate 37 g; Fat 14 g; Saturates 6 g

easy

15 mins

1 hr 5 mins

🧑‍🍳 **COOK'S TIP**

If you prefer, use slices of salami or Parma ham instead of the bacon, adding it to the dish 5 minutes before the end of the cooking time.

This is a classic potato dish of layered potatoes, cream, garlic, onion and cheese. Serve with pies, bakes and casseroles.

Potatoes Dauphinois

1 Lightly grease a 1-litre/1³/₄-pint shallow ovenproof dish with the butter.

2 Arrange a single layer of potato slices in the base of the prepared dish.

3 Top the potato slices with half the garlic, half the sliced red onion and one-third of the grated Gruyère cheese. Season to taste with salt and pepper.

4 Repeat these layers in exactly the same order, finishing with a layer of potatoes topped with the grated cheese.

5 Pour the cream over the top of the potatoes and cook in a preheated oven, 180°C/350°F/Gas Mark 4, for 1¹/₂ hours or until the potatoes are cooked through and the top is browned and crispy. Serve straight from the dish.

SERVES 4

15 g/¹/₂ oz butter
675 g/1 lb 8 oz waxy potatoes, sliced
2 garlic cloves, crushed
1 red onion, sliced
85 g/3 oz Gruyère cheese, grated
300 ml/10 fl oz double cream
salt and pepper

NUTRITION
Calories *580*; Sugars *5 g*; Protein *10 g*;
Carbohydrate *34 g*; Fat *46 g*; Saturates *28 g*

⭐⭐   easy
🕑   25 mins
🕐   1 hr 30 mins

 COOK'S TIP

There are many versions of this classic potato dish, but all contain double cream, making it a rich and very filling side dish or accompaniment. This recipe must be cooked in a shallow dish to ensure there is plenty of crispy topping.

This is a potato dish, which may be left to cook unattended while the remainder of the meal is being prepared, so it is ideal with stews.

Pommes Anna

SERVES 4

70 g/2½ oz butter, melted
675 g/1 lb 8 oz waxy potatoes
4 tbsp chopped mixed fresh herbs
salt and pepper
chopped fresh herbs, to garnish

1 Brush a 1-litre/1¾-pint ovenproof dish with a little of the melted butter.

2 Slice the potatoes thinly and pat dry with kitchen paper.

3 Arrange a layer of potato slices in the prepared dish until the base is covered. Brush with a little butter and sprinkle with one-quarter of the chopped mixed herbs. Season to taste with salt and pepper.

4 Continue layering the potato slices, brushing each layer with melted butter and sprinkling with herbs, until they are all used up.

5 Brush the top layer of potato slices with butter, cover the dish and cook in a preheated oven, 190°C/375°F/Gas Mark 5, for 1½ hours.

6 Transfer to a warmed ovenproof platter and return to the oven for a further 25–30 minutes until golden-brown. Garnish with chopped fresh herbs and serve immediately.

NUTRITION

Calories 237; Sugars 1 g; Protein 4 g;
Carbohydrate 29 g; Fat 13 g; Saturates 8 g

       easy

        15 mins

        2 hrs

 COOK'S TIP

Make sure that the potatoes are sliced very thinly so that they are almost transparent. This will ensure that they cook thoroughly.

This potato dish is cooked in the oven with leeks and wine. It is very quick and simple to make.

Casseroled Potatoes

1 Cook the potato chunks in a saucepan of boiling water for 5 minutes. Drain.

2 Meanwhile, melt the butter in a frying pan over a low heat. Add the leeks and sauté for 5 minutes or until they have softened.

3 Spoon the partially cooked potatoes and leeks into an ovenproof dish.

4 Mix the wine, vegetable stock, lemon juice and mixed herbs together in a measuring jug. Season to taste with salt and pepper, then pour the mixture over the potatoes and leeks.

5 Cook in a preheated oven, 190°C/375°F/Gas Mark 5, for 35 minutes or until the potatoes are tender.

6 Garnish the potato casserole with grated lemon rind and fresh herbs (if using) and serve as an accompaniment to meat casseroles or roast meat.

SERVES 4

675 g/1 lb 8 oz waxy potatoes, cut into chunks
1 tbsp butter
2 leeks, sliced
150 ml/5 fl oz dry white wine
150 ml/5 fl oz vegetable stock
1 tbsp lemon juice
2 tbsp chopped mixed fresh herbs
salt and pepper

to garnish
grated lemon rind
mixed fresh herbs, optional

NUTRITION
Calories *187*; Sugars *2 g*; Protein *4 g*;
Carbohydrate *31 g*; Fat *3 g*; Saturates *2 g*

⭐⭐ easy

🕐 10 mins

 50 mins

Liven up mashed potato by topping it with a crumble mixture flavoured with herbs, mustard and onion, which turns crunchy when it is baked.

Cheese Crumble-topped Mash

SERVES 4

900 g/2 lb floury potatoes, diced
25 g/1 oz butter
2 tbsp milk
50 g/1¾ oz mature Cheddar cheese or blue cheese, grated

crumble topping

40 g/1½ oz butter
1 onion, cut into chunks
1 garlic clove, crushed
1 tbsp wholegrain mustard
175 g/6 oz fresh wholemeal breadcrumbs
2 tbsp chopped fresh parsley
salt and pepper

NUTRITION
Calories 131; Sugars 1.4 g; Protein 3.8 g; Carbohydrate 17 g; Fat 5.7 g; Saturates 3.4 g

easy
10 mins
20–25 mins

1 Cook the potatoes in a saucepan of boiling water for 10 minutes or until cooked through completely.

2 Meanwhile, make the crumble topping. Melt the butter in a frying pan over a low heat. Add the onion, garlic and mustard and fry gently for 5 minutes, stirring constantly, until the onion chunks have softened.

3 Put the breadcrumbs and parsley into a mixing bowl and stir in the fried onion. Season to taste with salt and pepper.

4 Drain the potatoes thoroughly and place them in a mixing bowl. Add the butter and milk, then mash until smooth. Stir in the grated cheese while the mashed potato is still hot.

5 Spoon the mashed potato into a shallow ovenproof dish and sprinkle with the crumble topping.

6 Cook in a preheated oven, 200°C/400°F/Gas Mark 6, for 10–15 minutes until the crumble topping is golden-brown and crunchy. Serve immediately.

COOK'S TIP

For extra crunch, add some freshly cooked vegetables, such as celery and peppers, to the mashed potato at Step 4.

Hot soufflés have a reputation for being difficult to make, but this one is both simple and impressive. Make sure you serve the soufflé as soon as it is ready.

Carrot *and* Potato Soufflé

1 Brush the inside of an 850-ml/1½-pint soufflé dish with the butter. Sprinkle three-quarters of the breadcrumbs over the base and sides.

2 Cut the baked potatoes in half and scoop the flesh into a mixing bowl.

3 Add the carrots, egg yolks, orange juice and nutmeg to the potato flesh. Season to taste with salt and pepper.

4 Whisk the egg whites in a separate bowl until soft peaks form, then gently fold into the potato mixture with a metal spoon until well incorporated.

5 Gently spoon the potato and carrot mixture into the prepared soufflé dish. Sprinkle the remaining breadcrumbs over the top of the mixture.

6 Cook in a preheated oven, 200°C/400°F/Gas Mark 6, for 40 minutes until risen and golden. Do not open the oven door during the cooking time, otherwise the soufflé will sink. Garnish with carrot curls and serve.

SERVES 4

25 g/1 oz butter, melted
4 tbsp fresh wholemeal breadcrumbs
3 floury potatoes, baked in their skins
2 carrots, grated
2 eggs, separated
2 tbsp orange juice
¼ tsp freshly grated nutmeg
salt and pepper
carrot curls, to garnish

NUTRITION
Calories *294*; Sugars *6 g*; Protein *10 g*;
Carbohydrate *46 g*; Fat *9 g*; Saturates *4 g*

  easy

15 mins

40 mins

COOK'S TIP

To bake the potatoes, prick the skins with a fork and cook in a preheated oven, 190°C/375°F/Gas Mark 5, for about 1 hour.

This really is a great side dish, perfect for serving alongside main meals cooked in the oven.

Cheese *and* Potato Pie

SERVES 4

500 g/1 lb 2 oz potatoes
1 leek, sliced
3 garlic cloves, crushed
50 g/1¾ oz Cheddar cheese, grated
50 g/1¾ oz mozzarella cheese, grated
25 g/1 oz freshly grated Parmesan cheese
2 tbsp chopped fresh parsley
150 ml/5 fl oz single cream
150 ml/5 fl oz milk
salt and pepper
chopped flat-leaved parsley, to garnish

1 Cook the potatoes in a saucepan of boiling salted water for 10 minutes. Drain the potatoes thoroughly.

2 Cut the potatoes into thin slices. Arrange a layer of potatoes in the base of an ovenproof dish. Layer with a little of the leek, garlic, cheeses and parsley. Season to taste with salt and pepper.

3 Repeat the layers until all of the ingredients have been used, finishing with a layer of cheese. Mix the cream and milk together, season to taste with salt and pepper and pour over the potato layers.

4 Cook the pie in a preheated oven, 160°C/325°F/Gas Mark 3, for 1–1¼ hours or until the cheese is golden-brown and bubbling and the potatoes are tender.

5 Garnish with chopped fresh flat-leaved parsley and serve immediately.

NUTRITION
Calories *295*; Sugars *5 g*; Protein *13 g*;
Carbohydrate *24 g*; Fat *17 g*; Saturates *11 g*

 easy

 15 mins

1 hr 30 mins

🍳 **COOK'S TIP**

Potatoes make a very good basis for a vegetable accompaniment and combine well with a vast range of other ingredients. They are a good source of complex carbohydrate and contain a number of vitamins.

These puff pastries are ideal with a more formal meal because they take a short time to prepare and look really impressive.

Mini Vegetable Puff Pastries

1 Cut the pastry equally into 4 pieces. Roll each piece out on a lightly floured work surface to form a 13-cm/5-inch square. Place on a dampened baking tray and score a smaller 6-cm/2½-inch square inside.

2 Brush with beaten egg and cook in a preheated oven, 200°C/400°F/Gas Mark 6, for 20 minutes or until risen and golden-brown.

3 While the pastry is cooking, begin the filling. Cook the sweet potato in boiling water for 15 minutes, then drain. Blanch the asparagus in boiling water for 10 minutes or until tender. Drain and reserve.

4 Remove the pastry squares from the oven. Carefully cut out the central square of pastry, lift it out and reserve.

5 Melt the butter or margarine in a frying pan over a low heat. Add the leek and mushrooms and sauté for 2–3 minutes. Add the lime juice, thyme and mustard, season well with salt and pepper and stir in the sweet potatoes and asparagus. Spoon into the pastry cases, top with the reserved pastry squares and serve immediately.

S E R V E S   4

pastry cases
450 g/1 lb puff pastry
plain flour, for dusting
1 egg, beaten

filling
225 g/8 oz sweet potatoes, cubed
100 g/3½ oz baby asparagus spears
25 g/1 oz butter or margarine
1 leek, sliced
2 small open-cap mushrooms, sliced
1 tsp lime juice
1 tsp chopped fresh thyme
pinch of dried mustard
salt and pepper

N U T R I T I O N
Calories *210*; Sugars *2 g*; Protein *4 g*;
Carbohydrate *21 g*; Fat *13 g*; Saturates *1.7 g*

 easy

 15 mins

15 mins

25 mins

🍳 **C O O K ' S   T I P**

Use a colourful selection of any vegetables you have at hand for this recipe.

Although virtually unknown in India, this dish is a very popular item on Indian restaurant menus in other parts of the world.

Bombay Potatoes

SERVES 4

1 kg/2 lb 4 oz waxy potatoes
2 tbsp ghee or vegetable oil
1 tsp panch poran spice mix
3 tsp ground turmeric
2 tbsp tomato purée
300 ml/10 fl oz natural yogurt
salt
chopped fresh coriander, to garnish

1 Put the whole potatoes into a large saucepan of salted cold water, bring to the boil, then simmer until the potatoes are just cooked, but not tender. The time depends on the size of the potato, but an average-sized one should take about 15 minutes.

2 Heat the ghee in a saucepan over a medium heat. Add the panch poran, turmeric, tomato purée, yogurt and salt. Bring to the boil and simmer, uncovered, for 5 minutes.

3 Drain the potatoes and cut each one into 4 pieces. Add the potatoes to the pan, cover and cook briefly. Transfer to an ovenproof casserole, cover and cook in a preheated oven, 180°C/350°F/Gas Mark 4, for about 40 minutes or until the potatoes are tender and the sauce has thickened slightly.

4 Transfer the potatoes to a serving dish, sprinkle with chopped coriander and serve immediately.

NUTRITION
Calories 307; Sugars 9 g; Protein 9 g;
Carbohydrate 51 g; Fat 9 g; Saturates 5 g

    very easy

5 mins

1 hr 10 mins

COOK'S TIP

Panch poran spice mix can be bought from Asian or Indian grocer shops, or make your own from equal quantities of cumin seeds, fennel seeds, mustard seeds, nigella seeds and fenugreek seeds.

In this classic French recipe, sliced potatoes are cooked with onions to make a delicious accompaniment to a main meal.

Potatoes Lyonnaise

1 Cut the potatoes into 5-mm/¼-inch slices. Cook the sliced potatoes in a large saucepan of lightly salted boiling water for about 10–12 minutes until just tender. Avoid boiling too rapidly or the potatoes will break up and lose their shape. When cooked, drain well.

2 While the potatoes are cooking, heat the olive oil and butter in a very large frying pan over a medium heat. Add the onions and garlic (if using) and fry, stirring frequently, until the onions are softened.

3 Add the cooked potato to the frying pan and cook with the onions, stirring occasionally, for about 5–8 minutes until the potatoes are well browned.

4 Season to taste with salt and pepper. Sprinkle over the chopped parsley to serve. If wished, transfer the potatoes and onions to a large ovenproof dish and keep warm in a low oven until ready to serve.

SERVES 4

1.25 kg/2 lb 12 oz potatoes
4 tbsp olive oil
25 g/1 oz butter
2 onions, sliced
2–3 garlic cloves, crushed (optional)
salt and pepper
chopped fresh parsley, to garnish

NUTRITION
Calories 277; Sugars 4 g; Protein 5 g; Carbohydrate 40 g; Fat 12 g; Saturates 4 g

⭐ very easy
🕐 10 mins
🕐 25 mins

 COOK'S TIP

If the potatoes blacken slightly as they are boiling, add a spoonful of lemon juice to the cooking water.

Warm new potatoes, served in a choice of three delicious dressings, make a delightful variation to the usual potato salad. The nutritional information is for the light curry dressing.

Three-way Potato Salad

SERVES 4

500 g/1 lb 2 oz new potatoes for each dressing
salt and pepper
mixed fresh herbs, to garnish

light curry dressing
1 tbsp vegetable oil
1 tbsp medium curry paste
1 small onion, chopped
1 tbsp mango chutney, chopped
6 tbsp natural yogurt
3 tbsp single cream, plus extra to garnish
2 tbsp mayonnaise

vinaigrette dressing
6 tbsp hazelnut oil
3 tbsp cider vinegar
1 tsp wholegrain mustard
1 tsp caster sugar
few fresh basil leaves, torn

parsley cream
3 tbsp low-fat mayonnaise
150 ml/5 fl oz soured cream
4 spring onions, chopped finely
1 tbsp chopped fresh parsley

NUTRITION
Calories *310*; Sugars *12 g*; Protein *6 g*;
Carbohydrate *31 g*; Fat *19 g*; Saturates *4 g*

very easy

10–20 mins

20 mins

1 To make the light curry dressing, heat the vegetable oil in a saucepan over a low heat. Add the curry paste and onion and fry, stirring frequently, until the onion has softened. Remove from the heat and leave to cool slightly.

2 Mix the mango chutney, yogurt, cream and mayonnaise together. Add the curry mixture and blend together. Season to taste with salt and pepper.

3 To make the vinaigrette dressing, whisk the hazelnut oil, vinegar, mustard, sugar and basil in a small bowl. Season to taste with salt and pepper.

4 To make the parsley cream, mix the mayonnaise, soured cream, spring onions and parsley together. Season to taste with salt and pepper.

5 Cook the potatoes in lightly salted boiling water until just tender. Drain well and leave to cool for 5 minutes, then add the chosen dressing, tossing to coat. Serve, garnished with fresh herbs, spooning 1 tablespoon of cream on to the potatoes if you have used the curry dressing.

Earthy potatoes are delicious when served in a tangy spicy tomatillo sauce and sprinkled with plenty of fresh coriander.

Potatoes *in* Green Sauce

1 Cook the potatoes in a saucepan of salted boiling water for about 15 minutes or until almost tender. Do not overcook them. Drain thoroughly and reserve.

2 Meanwhile, lightly char the onion, garlic, chilli and tomatillos or tomatoes in a heavy-based, ungreased frying pan. Leave to cool and, when cool enough to handle, peel and chop the onion, garlic and chilli. Chop the tomatillos or tomatoes. Put into a food processor or blender with half the stock and process to form a purée. Add the cumin, thyme and oregano.

3 Heat the vegetable oil in the heavy-based frying pan over a low heat. Add the purée and cook for 5 minutes, stirring, to reduce slightly and concentrate the flavours.

4 Add the potatoes and courgette to the purée and pour in the rest of the stock. Add about half of the coriander and cook for a further 5 minutes or until the courgette pieces are tender.

5 Transfer to a serving bowl and serve sprinkled with the remaining chopped coriander to garnish.

SERVES 4

1 kg/2 lb 4 oz small waxy potatoes, peeled
1 onion, halved and unpeeled
8 garlic cloves, unpeeled
1 fresh green chilli
8 tomatillos, outer husks removed, or small tart tomatoes
225 ml/8 fl oz chicken, meat or vegetable stock, preferably home-made
1 tsp ground cumin
1 fresh thyme sprig or good pinch of dried
1 fresh oregano sprig or good pinch of dried
2 tbsp vegetable or extra virgin olive oil
1 courgette, chopped roughly
1 bunch of fresh coriander, chopped
salt

NUTRITION
Calories *61*; Sugars *1.4 g*; Protein *2 g*; Carbohydrate *11 g*; Fat *1.4 g*; Saturates *0.2 g*

★★ easy
🌀 5 mins
🕐 25 mins

 COOK'S TIP

If fresh coriander is unavailable, substitute with flat-leaved parsley.

Serve these as an accompaniment to other barbecue dishes or with a spicy dip as nibbles while the main dishes are being cooked.

Spicy Sweet Potato Slices

SERVES 4

450 g/1 lb sweet potatoes, unpeeled
2 tbsp sunflower oil
1 tsp chilli sauce
salt and pepper

1 Bring a large saucepan of water to the boil over a medium heat. Add the sweet potatoes and parboil them for 10 minutes. Drain the potatoes thoroughly and transfer to a chopping board.

2 Peel the potatoes and cut them into thick slices.

3 To make the coating for the potatoes, mix the sunflower oil, chilli sauce and salt and pepper to taste together in a small bowl.

4 Brush the spicy mixture liberally over one side of the potatoes. Transfer the potatoes to a lit barbecue and place, oil side down, over medium–hot coals. Cook them for 5–6 minutes.

5 Lightly brush the tops of the potatoes with the oil, turn them over and cook them for a further 5 minutes or until crisp and golden.

6 Transfer the potatoes to a warm serving dish and serve immediately.

NUTRITION
Calories *178*; Sugars *1 g*; Protein *2 g*;
Carbohydrate *32 g*; Fat *6 g*; Saturates *0.7 g*

⭐⭐ easy
🕐 10 mins
🕐 25 mins

🍴 **COOK'S TIP**

For a simple dip to accompany the potatoes combine 150 ml/5 fl oz soured cream with ½ teaspoon of sugar, ½ teaspoon of Dijon mustard and salt and pepper to taste. Leave to chill until required.

Serve this delicious barbecued potato dish with barbecued kebabs, bean burgers or sausages.

Garlic Potato Wedges

1 Bring a large saucepan of water to the boil over a medium heat. Add the potatoes and parboil them for 10 minutes. Drain the potatoes, refresh under cold running water and drain again thoroughly.

2 Transfer the potatoes to a chopping board and leave to cool. When cool enough to handle, cut them into thick wedges, but do not peel.

3 Heat the olive oil and butter in a small frying pan together with the garlic. Cook gently until the garlic begins to brown, then remove from the heat.

4 Stir the herbs and seasoning into the mixture in the pan.

5 Brush the herb and butter mixture all over the potato wedges.

6 Transfer the potatoes to a lit barbecue and cook over hot coals for about 10–15 minutes, brushing liberally with any of the remaining herb and butter mixture or until the potato wedges are just tender.

7 Transfer the garlic potato wedges to a warmed serving plate and serve as a starter or as a side dish.

SERVES 4

3 large baking potatoes, scrubbed
4 tbsp olive oil
2 tbsp butter
2 garlic cloves, chopped
1 tbsp chopped fresh rosemary
1 tbsp chopped fresh parsley
1 tbsp chopped fresh thyme
salt and pepper

NUTRITION
Calories *257*; Sugars *1 g*; Protein *3 g*;
Carbohydrate *26 g*; Fat *16 g*; Saturates *5 g*

 very easy

 10 mins

30–35 mins

 COOK'S TIP

You may find it easier to barbecue these potatoes in a hinged rack or in a specially designed barbecue roasting tray.

Vegetarian *and* Vegan Suppers

The potato has become a valued staple of the vegetarian diet, yet anyone who thought this would make for dull eating will be pleasantly surprised by the rich variety of dishes in this section. In addition to traditional hearty bakes and hotpots, there are also influences from around the world in dishes such as Tofu & Vegetable Stir-fry from China, and Potato & Vegetable Curry from India. They all make exciting eating at any time of year.

This quick one-pot dish is ideal for a snack. Packed with colour and flavour, it is very versatile because you can add other vegetables to taste.

Pepper *and* Mushroom Hash

SERVES 4

675 g/1 lb 8 oz potatoes, cubed
1 tbsp olive oil
2 garlic cloves, crushed
1 green pepper, deseeded and cubed
1 yellow pepper, deseeded and cubed
3 tomatoes, diced
75 g/2³⁄₄ oz button mushrooms, halved
1 tbsp Worcestershire sauce
2 tbsp chopped fresh basil
salt and pepper
fresh basil leaves, to garnish

1 Cook the potatoes in a saucepan of boiling salted water for 7–8 minutes. Drain well and reserve.

2 Heat the olive oil in a large, heavy-based frying pan over a medium heat. Add the potatoes and cook, stirring constantly, for 8–10 minutes until browned.

3 Add the garlic and peppers and cook, stirring frequently, for 2–3 minutes.

4 Stir in the tomatoes and mushrooms and cook, stirring, for 5–6 minutes.

5 Stir in the Worcestershire sauce and basil and season to taste with salt and pepper. Transfer to a warmed serving dish, garnish with basil and serve.

NUTRITION

Calories *182*; Sugars *6 g*; Protein *5 g*;
Carbohydrate *34 g*; Fat *4 g*; Saturates *0.5 g*

⭐⭐ easy
🕐 5 mins
🕐 30 mins

 COOK'S TIP

Most brands of Worcestershire sauce contain anchovies, so if you are a vegetarian check the label to make sure you choose a vegetarian variety.

Very little meat is eaten in India, and the Indian diet is mainly vegetarian. This potato curry with added vegetables makes a substantial main meal.

Potato *and* Vegetable Curry

1 Heat the vegetable oil in a large heavy-based saucepan or frying pan over a low heat. Add the potato chunks, onions and garlic and fry, stirring frequently, for 2–3 minutes.

2 Add the garam masala, turmeric, ground cumin, ground coriander, ginger and chilli to the pan, mixing the spices into the vegetables. Fry over a low heat, stirring constantly, for 1 minute.

3 Add the cauliflower florets, tomatoes, peas, coriander and vegetable stock to the curry mixture.

4 Cook the potato curry over a low heat for 30–40 minutes or until the potatoes are tender and completely cooked through.

5 Garnish the potato curry with fresh coriander and serve with plain boiled rice or warm Indian bread.

SERVES 4

4 tbsp vegetable oil
675 g/1 lb 8 oz waxy potatoes, cut into large chunks
2 onions, quartered
3 garlic cloves, crushed
1 tsp garam masala
½ tsp turmeric
½ tsp ground cumin
½ tsp ground coriander
2 tsp grated fresh root ginger
1 fresh red chilli, chopped
225 g/8 oz cauliflower florets
4 tomatoes, peeled and quartered
75 g/2¾ oz frozen peas
2 tbsp chopped fresh coriander
300 ml/10 fl oz vegetable stock
shredded fresh coriander, to garnish
boiled rice or warm Indian bread, to serve

NUTRITION

Calories *301*; Sugars *10 g*; Protein *9 g*; Carbohydrate *41 g*; Fat *12 g*; Saturates *1 g*

 COOK'S TIP

Use a large heavy-based saucepan or frying pan for this recipe to ensure that the potatoes are cooked thoroughly.

⭐⭐ easy
🕐 5 mins
🕐 45 mins

Fried mashed potato and leftover greens is best known as Bubble and Squeak. It is served as an accompaniment.

Bubble *and* Squeak

SERVES 4

450 g/1 lb floury potatoes, diced
225 g/8 oz Savoy cabbage, shredded
5 tbsp vegetable oil
2 leeks, chopped
1 garlic clove, crushed
225 g/8 oz smoked tofu, drained and cubed
salt and pepper
shredded cooked leek, to garnish

1 Cook the diced potatoes in a saucepan of lightly salted boiling water for 10 minutes until tender. Drain and mash the potatoes.

2 Meanwhile, blanch the cabbage in a separate saucepan of boiling water for 5 minutes. Drain well and add to the potato.

3 Heat the oil in a heavy-based frying pan over a low heat. Add the leeks and garlic and fry for 2–3 minutes. Stir into the potato and cabbage mixture.

4 Add the smoked tofu and season well with salt and pepper. Cook over a medium heat for 10 minutes.

5 Carefully turn the whole mixture over and continue to cook over a medium heat for a further 5–7 minutes until crispy underneath. Transfer to a large serving dish, garnish with shredded leek and serve immediately.

NUTRITION
Calories 301; Sugars 5 g; Protein 11 g;
Carbohydrate 24 g; Fat 18 g; Saturates 2 g

✪✪   easy
◔   15 mins
◕   40 mins

 COOK'S TIP

This version of the classic recipe is a perfect main meal, because the smoked tofu cubes added to the basic Bubble and Squeak mixture make it very substantial and nourishing.

These cakes, made from a spicy vegetable mixture, are delightfully easy to make and taste delicious.

Spicy Vegetable Cakes

1 Place the potatoes, onion and cauliflower florets in a saucepan of water and bring to the boil. Reduce the heat and simmer until the potatoes are cooked through. Remove the vegetables from the pan with a slotted spoon and drain thoroughly. Reserve.

2 Add the peas and spinach purée to the vegetables and mix, mashing down thoroughly with a fork.

3 Finely chop the green chillies and the fresh coriander leaves.

4 Mix the chillies and fresh coriander leaves with the ginger, garlic, ground coriander, turmeric and salt.

5 Blend this mixture into the vegetables, mixing with a fork to make a paste.

6 Scatter the breadcrumbs on to a large plate.

7 Break off 10–12 small balls from the spice paste. Flatten them with the palm of your hand or with a palette knife to make flat, round shapes.

8 Dip each cake in the breadcrumbs, coating well.

9 Heat the vegetable oil in a heavy-based frying-pan over a medium heat. Add the vegetable cakes, in batches, and fry until golden-brown, turning occasionally. Transfer to serving plates and garnish with fresh chilli strips and a few sprigs of fresh coriander. Serve hot.

MAKES 12

600 g/1 lb 5 oz potatoes, sliced
1 medium onion, sliced
½ medium cauliflower, cut into small florets
50 g/1¾ oz cooked peas
1 tbsp spinach purée
2–3 fresh green chillies
1 tbsp fresh coriander leaves
1 tsp finely chopped fresh root ginger
1 tsp crushed garlic
1 tsp ground coriander
pinch of turmeric
1 tsp salt
50 g/1¾ oz breadcrumbs
300 ml/10 fl oz vegetable oil

to garnish
fresh chilli strips
fresh coriander sprigs

NUTRITION

Calories *268*; Sugars *1 g*; Protein *2 g*; Carbohydrate *9 g*; Fat *25 g*; Saturates *3 g*

⭐⭐   easy

🖐   20 mins

    25 mins

This curry is very popular in India. There are many different ways of cooking chickpeas, but this spicy version is probably one of the most delicious.

Chickpea Curry

SERVES 4

6 tbsp vegetable oil
2 onions, sliced
1 tsp finely chopped fresh root ginger
1 tsp ground cumin
1 tsp ground coriander
1 tsp fresh garlic, crushed
1 tsp chilli powder
2 fresh green chillies
1 tbsp fresh coriander leaves
150 ml/5 fl oz water
300 g/10½ oz potatoes
400 g/14 oz canned chickpeas, drained
1 tbsp lemon juice
chapatis to serve (optional)

1 Heat the vegetable oil in a large saucepan over a medium heat.

2 Add the onions and fry, stirring occasionally, until golden-brown.

3 Reduce the heat, add the ginger, ground cumin, ground coriander, garlic, chilli powder, fresh green chillies and fresh coriander leaves to the pan and stir-fry for 2 minutes.

4 Add the water to the mixture in the pan and stir to mix.

5 Using a sharp knife, cut the potato into small cubes.

6 Add the potatoes and the drained chickpeas to the mixture in the pan, cover and leave to simmer, stirring occasionally, for 5–7 minutes.

7 Sprinkle the lemon juice over the curry.

8 Transfer the chickpea curry to 4 large serving dishes. Serve the curry hot with chapatis, if you wish.

NUTRITION

Calories 114; Sugars 2 g; Protein 3 g;
Carbohydrate 10 g; Fat 7 g; Saturates 0.7 g

 moderate

5–10 mins

15 mins

COOK'S TIP

Using canned chickpeas saves time, but you can use dried chickpeas, if you prefer. Soak them overnight, then boil them for 15–20 minutes or until soft.

This bread can be quite rich and is usually made for special occasions. It can be eaten on its own or with a vegetable curry.

Vegetable-stuffed Paratas

1 To make the paratas, mix the flour, salt, water and ghee to form a dough.

2 Divide the dough equally into 6–8 portions. Roll each portion out on to a floured work surface. Brush the centre of the dough portions with ½ teaspoon of ghee. Fold the dough portions in half, roll into a pipe-like shape, flatten with the palms of your hands, then roll around a finger to form a coil. Roll out again, using flour to dust when necessary, to form a round about 18 cm/7 inches in diameter.

3 Place the potatoes in a saucepan of boiling water and cook until soft. Drain thoroughly, then mash. Reserve.

4 Blend the turmeric, garam masala, ginger, coriander leaves, chillies and salt together in a bowl.

5 Add the spice mixture to the mashed potato and mix well. Spread about 1 tablespoon of the spicy potato mixture on each dough portion and cover with another rolled-out piece of dough. Seal the edges well.

6 Heat 2 teaspoons of ghee in a heavy-based frying pan over a medium heat. Place the paratas gently in the pan, in batches, and fry, turning and moving them about gently with a flat spoon until golden.

7 Remove the paratas from the frying pan and serve immediately.

SERVES 4

dough
225 g/8 oz wholemeal flour (ata or chapati flour), plus extra for dusting
½ tsp salt
200 ml/7 fl oz water
100 g/3½ oz ghee
2½ tbsp ghee, for frying

filling
675 g/1 lb 8 oz potatoes
½ tsp turmeric
1 tsp garam masala
1 tsp finely chopped fresh root ginger
1 tbsp fresh coriander leaves
3 fresh green chillies, chopped finely
1 tsp salt

NUTRITION
Calories *391*; Sugars *2 g*; Protein *6 g*;
Carbohydrate *40 g*; Fat *24 g*; Saturates *2.5 g*

 moderate

25 mins

30–35 mins

Pakoras are eaten all over India. They are made in many different ways and with a variety of fillings. Sometimes they are served with yogurt.

Pakoras

SERVES 4

6 tbsp gram flour
½ tsp salt
1 tsp chilli powder
1 tsp baking powder
1½ tsp white cumin seeds
1 tsp pomegranate seeds
300 ml/10 fl oz water
1 tbsp finely chopped fresh coriander
vegetables of your choice: cauliflower cut into small florets, onions cut into rings, sliced potatoes, sliced aubergines or fresh spinach leaves
600 ml/1 pint vegetable oil, for deep-frying
1 fresh coriander sprig, to garnish

NUTRITION
Calories 331; Sugars 5 g; Protein 9 g;
Carbohydrate 27 g; Fat 22 g; Saturates 3 g

     very easy

     15 mins

     15–20 mins

1 Sift the gram flour into a large mixing bowl. Add the salt, chilli powder, baking powder, cumin and pomegranate seeds and blend together well. Pour in the water and beat thoroughly to form a smooth batter.

2 Add the chopped coriander leaves and mix. Set the batter aside.

3 Dip the prepared vegetables of your choice into the batter, carefully shaking off any excess batter.

4 Heat the vegetable oil in a large heavy-based saucepan to 180°C/350°F or until a cube of bread browns in 30 seconds. Place the batter-coated vegetables of your choice in the oil and deep-fry, in batches, turning once.

5 Repeat this process until all of the batter has been used up.

6 Transfer the vegetables to kitchen paper and drain. Transfer to a large serving plate, garnish with a sprig of fresh coriander and serve immediately.

COOK'S TIP

When deep-frying, it is important to use oil at the correct temperature. If the oil is too hot, the outside of the food will burn, as will the spices, before the inside is cooked. If the oil is too cool, the food will be sodden with oil.

This is based on a Moroccan dish in which potatoes are spiced with coriander and cumin and cooked in a lemon sauce.

Potato *and* Lemon Casserole

1 Heat the olive oil in a flameproof casserole over a medium heat. Add the onion and sauté, stirring frequently, for 3 minutes.

2 Add the garlic and cook for 30 seconds. Stir in the spices and cook, stirring constantly, for 1 minute.

3 Add the carrot, turnips, courgette and potatoes and stir to coat in the oil.

4 Add the lemon juice and rind and the vegetable stock. Season to taste with salt and pepper. Cover and cook over a medium heat, stirring occasionally, for 20–30 minutes until tender.

5 Remove the lid, sprinkle in the coriander and stir well. Serve immediately.

SERVES 4

100 ml/3½ fl oz olive oil
2 red onions, cut into 8 pieces
3 garlic cloves, crushed
2 tsp ground cumin
2 tsp ground coriander
pinch of cayenne pepper
1 carrot, sliced thickly
2 small turnips, quartered
1 courgette, sliced
500 g/1 lb 2 oz potatoes, sliced thickly
juice and grated rind of 2 large lemons
300 ml/10 fl oz vegetable stock
2 tbsp chopped fresh coriander
salt and pepper

NUTRITION
Calories *338*; Sugars *8 g*; Protein *5 g*;
Carbohydrate *29 g*; Fat *23 g*; Saturates *2 g*

 easy
 15 mins
15 mins
35 mins

COOK'S TIP

Check the vegetables while they are cooking, because they may begin to stick to the pan. Add a little more boiling water or stock, if necessary.

This is a quick dish to prepare, making it ideal as a mid-week supper dish, after a busy day at work!

Tofu *and* Vegetable Stir-fry

SERVES 4

175 g/6 oz potatoes, cubed
1 tbsp vegetable oil
1 red onion, sliced
225 g/8 oz firm tofu, drained and diced
2 courgettes, diced
8 canned artichoke hearts, halved
150 ml/5 fl oz passata
1 tbsp sweet chilli sauce
1 tbsp soy sauce
1 tsp caster sugar
2 tbsp chopped fresh basil
salt and pepper

1 Cook the potatoes in a saucepan of boiling water for 10 minutes. Drain thoroughly and reserve until required.

2 Heat the vegetable oil in a preheated wok or large frying pan over a medium heat. Add the red onion and sauté for 2 minutes or until the onion has softened, stirring.

3 Stir the tofu and courgettes into the softened onion and cook for 3–4 minutes until they begin to brown slightly.

4 Add the cooked potatoes to the wok or frying pan, stirring to mix.

5 Stir in the artichoke hearts, passata, sweet chilli sauce, soy sauce, sugar and chopped fresh basil.

6 Season to taste with salt and pepper and cook for a further 5 minutes, stirring well.

7 Transfer the stir-fry to 4 serving dishes and serve immediately.

NUTRITION
Calories *124*; Sugars *2 g*; Protein *6 g*;
Carbohydrate *11 g*; Fat *6 g*; Saturates *1 g*

★★★   moderate
🕐   5 mins
🕐   25 mins

 COOK'S TIP

Canned artichoke hearts should be drained thoroughly and rinsed before use because they often have salt added.

Enticing little tasty mouthfuls of sweet potato, served hot and sizzling from the pan with a delicious fresh tomato sauce.

Sweet Potato Cakes

1 To make the soy-tomato sauce, heat the vegetable oil in a preheated wok over a medium heat. Add the garlic and ginger and stir-fry for 1 minute. Add the tomatoes and stir-fry for a further 2 minutes. Remove from the heat and stir in the soy sauce, lime juice and coriander. Reserve and keep warm.

2 Peel the sweet potatoes and grate finely. Place the garlic, chilli and coriander in a mortar and crush to a smooth paste with a pestle. Stir in the soy sauce and mix with the sweet potatoes.

3 Divide the mixture equally into 12 portions. Dip them into the flour and pat into a flat, round patty shape.

4 Heat a shallow layer of vegetable oil in a wide frying pan over a high heat. Add the sweet potato patties, in batches, and fry until golden, turning once.

5 Drain on kitchen paper and sprinkle with sesame seeds. Transfer to a serving plate, garnish with a few sprigs of fresh herbs and serve hot with a spoonful of the soy-tomato sauce.

SERVES 4

500 g/1 lb 2 oz sweet potatoes
2 garlic cloves, crushed
1 small fresh green chilli, chopped
2 fresh coriander sprigs, chopped
1 tbsp dark soy sauce
plain flour, for shaping
125 ml/4 fl oz vegetable oil, for shallow-frying
sesame seeds, for sprinkling
fresh herb sprigs, to garnish

soy-tomato sauce
2 tsp vegetable oil
1 garlic clove, chopped finely
1½ tsp finely chopped fresh root ginger
3 tomatoes, peeled and chopped
2 tbsp dark soy sauce
1 tbsp lime juice
2 tbsp chopped fresh coriander

NUTRITION
Calories *349*; Sugars *9 g*; Protein *4 g*; Carbohydrate *32 g*; Fat *24 g*; Saturates *3 g*

easy

10–15 mins

15 mins

Vegetable
Savouries

The recipes in this section prove that meat does not have to be involved in a truly excellent main meal. You will find dishes with an international flavour, such as Potato & Spinach Gnocchi from Italy, and Potato & Aubergine Gratin, similar to Moussaka, from Greece. Family favourites such as Nutty Harvest Loaf, and Vegetable Hotpot, have been included, while the needs of the dinner party have not been forgotten with the spectacular Three Cheese Soufflé. Whatever the occasion, you are sure to find something here to satisfy the heartiest of appetites.

POTATOES

Sweet potatoes have very dense flesh and a delicious, sweet, earthy taste, which contrasts well with the flavour of the ginger.

Sweet Potato *and* Leek Patties

SERVES 4

900 g/2 lb sweet potatoes
4 tsp sunflower oil
2 leeks, trimmed and finely chopped
1 garlic clove, crushed
2 tsp finely chopped fresh root ginger
200 g/7 oz canned sweetcorn, drained
2 tbsp low-fat natural fromage frais
6 tbsp wholemeal flour
salt and pepper

ginger sauce
2 tbsp white wine vinegar
2 tsp caster sugar
1 fresh red chilli, deseeded and chopped
2.5-cm/1-inch piece of fresh root ginger,
   cut into thin strips
2 tbsp ginger wine
4 tbsp vegetable stock
1 tsp cornflour

to serve
lettuce leaves
spring onions, shredded

NUTRITION
Calories *403*; Sugars *34 g*; Protein *8 g*;
Carbohydrate *67 g*; Fat *12 g*; Saturates *2 g*

moderate

45 mins

40 mins

1 Peel the sweet potatoes, cut into thick cubes and cook in a saucepan of boiling water for 10–15 minutes. Drain well and mash. Leave to cool.

2 Heat 2 teaspoons of the sunflower oil in a large frying pan over a medium-low heat. Add the leeks, garlic and ginger and fry for 2–3 minutes. Stir into the potato with the sweetcorn, seasoning and fromage frais. Form into 8 patties and toss in the flour. Leave to chill for 30 minutes. Place the patties on a grill rack and lightly brush with sunflower oil. Cook under a preheated hot grill for 5 minutes, then turn over, brush with oil and cook for a further 5 minutes.

3 To make the sauce, place the vinegar, sugar, chilli and ginger in a saucepan and simmer for 5 minutes. Stir in the wine. Blend the stock and cornflour together and add to the sauce, stirring until thickened. Serve the patties with lettuce and spring onions, and the sauce.

COOK'S TIP

If you prefer, use petit pois instead of the canned sweetcorn. Cook them first if they are frozen.

Ratatouille is a classic dish of vegetables cooked in a tomato and herb sauce. Here it is topped with diced potatoes and cheese.

Ratatouille Vegetable Grill

1 Peel and finely chop the onions and garlic. Rinse, deseed and slice the peppers. Rinse, trim and cut the aubergine into small cubes. Rinse, trim and thinly slice the courgettes.

2 Place the onion, garlic and peppers in a large saucepan. Add the tomatoes, and stir in the bouquet garni, tomato purée and salt and pepper to taste. Bring to the boil, cover and simmer for 10 minutes, stirring halfway through. Stir in the prepared aubergine and courgettes and cook, uncovered, for a further 10 minutes, stirring occasionally.

3 Meanwhile, cut the potatoes into 2.5-cm/1-inch cubes. Place the potatoes into another saucepan and cover with water. Bring to the boil and cook for 10–12 minutes until tender. Drain and reserve.

4 Transfer the vegetables to a heatproof gratin dish. Arrange the cooked potatoes evenly over the vegetables.

5 Sprinkle the grated Cheddar cheese over the potatoes and place under a preheated medium–hot grill for 5 minutes until golden, bubbling and hot. Serve garnished with snipped chives.

SERVES 4

2 onions
1 garlic clove
1 red pepper
1 green pepper
1 aubergine
2 courgettes
800 g/1 lb 12 oz canned chopped tomatoes
1 bouquet garni
2 tbsp tomato purée
900 g/2 lb potatoes
75 g/2¾ oz reduced-fat mature Cheddar cheese, grated
salt and pepper
2 tbsp snipped fresh chives, to garnish

NUTRITION
Calories *287*; Sugars *13 g*; Protein *14 g*; Carbohydrate *53 g*; Fat *4 g*; Saturates *2 g*

⭐⭐⭐⭐ challenging
🌀 15 mins
🕐 25 mins

 COOK'S TIP

You can vary the vegetables in this dish depending on seasonal availability and personal preference. Try broccoli, carrots or sweetcorn, if you prefer.

Potatoes make a great pizza base and this recipe is well worth making, rather than using a ready-made base, both for texture and flavour.

Potato *and* Pepperoni Pizza

SERVES 4

1 tbsp butter, plus extra for greasing
1–2 tbsp plain flour, for dusting
900 g/2 lb floury potatoes, diced
2 garlic cloves, crushed
2 tbsp chopped mixed fresh herbs
1 egg, beaten
6 tbsp passata
2 tbsp tomato purée
50 g/1¾ oz pepperoni slices
1 green pepper, cut into strips
1 yellow pepper, cut into strips
2 large open-cap mushrooms, sliced
25 g/1 oz stoned black olives, quartered
125 g/4½ oz mozzarella cheese, sliced

1 Grease and flour a 23-cm/9-inch pizza tin.

2 Cook the diced potatoes in a saucepan of boiling water for 10 minutes or until cooked through. Drain and mash until smooth. Transfer the mashed potato to a mixing bowl and stir in the butter, garlic, herbs and egg.

3 Spread the mixture into the prepared pizza tin. Cook in a preheated oven, 220°C/425°F/Gas Mark 7, for 7–10 minutes or until the pizza base begins to set.

4 Mix the passata and tomato purée together and spoon this over the pizza base, to within 1 cm/½ inch of the edge of the base.

5 Arrange the pepperoni slices and the peppers, mushrooms and olives evenly on top of the passata.

6 Scatter the mozzarella cheese on top of the pizza. Return to the oven for 20 minutes or until the base is cooked through and the cheese has melted.

NUTRITION
Calories 234; Sugars 5 g; Protein 4 g;
Carbohydrate 30 g; Fat 12 g; Saturates 1 g

★★★ moderate
 20 mins
🕐 45 mins

🧑‍🍳 COOK'S TIP

This pizza base is softer in texture than a normal bread dough and is ideal served from the tin. Top with any of your favourite pizza ingredients.

These small potato dumplings are flavoured with spinach, cooked in boiling water and served with a tomato sauce.

Potato *and* Spinach Gnocchi

1 Cook the diced potatoes in a saucepan of boiling water for 10 minutes or until cooked through. Drain thoroughly, then mash the potatoes.

2 Meanwhile, blanch the spinach in a saucepan of boiling water for about 1–2 minutes. Drain the spinach and shred the leaves.

3 Transfer the mashed potato to a lightly floured chopping board and make a well in the centre. Add the egg yolk, olive oil, spinach, salt and pepper and a little of the flour and quickly mix the ingredients into the potato, adding more flour as you go, until you have a firm dough. Divide the mixture into very small dumplings.

4 Cook the gnocchi, in batches, in a saucepan of boiling salted water for about 5 minutes or until they rise to the surface.

5 Meanwhile, to make the sauce, put the olive oil, shallots, garlic, passata and sugar into a saucepan and cook over a low heat for 10–15 minutes or until the sauce has thickened.

6 Drain the gnocchi, using a slotted spoon and transfer to 4 warmed serving dishes. Spoon over the sauce and garnish with baby spinach leaves.

 COOK'S TIP

Add chopped fresh herbs and cheese to the gnocchi dough instead of the spinach, if you prefer.

SERVES 4

300 g/10½ oz floury potatoes, diced
175 g/6 oz fresh spinach
1 egg yolk
1 tsp olive oil
125 g/4½ oz plain flour, plus extra for dusting
salt and pepper
baby spinach leaves, to garnish

sauce
1 tbsp olive oil
2 shallots, chopped
1 garlic clove, crushed
300 ml/10 fl oz passata
2 tsp soft light brown sugar

NUTRITION
Calories 315; Sugars 7 g; Protein 8 g; Carbohydrate 56 g; Fat 8 g; Saturates 1 g

 moderate
20 mins
30 mins

This is a very colourful and nutritious dish, packed full of crunchy vegetables in a tasty white wine sauce.

Potato-topped Vegetables

S E R V E S 4

1 carrot, diced
175 g/6 oz cauliflower florets
175 g/6 oz broccoli florets
1 fennel bulb, sliced
75 g/2³/₄ oz French beans, halved
25 g/1 oz butter
2¹/₂ tbsp plain flour
150 ml/5 fl oz vegetable stock
150 ml/5 fl oz dry white wine
150 ml/5 fl oz milk
175 g/6 oz chestnut mushrooms, quartered
2 tbsp chopped fresh sage

topping
900 g/2 lb floury potatoes, diced
25 g/1 oz butter
4 tbsp natural yogurt
70 g/2¹/₂ oz freshly grated Parmesan cheese
1 tsp fennel seeds
salt and pepper

N U T R I T I O N
Calories 413; Sugars 11 g; Protein 19 g;
Carbohydrate 41 g; Fat 18 g; Saturates 11 g

⭐⭐⭐   moderate
🕐   20 mins
🕐   1 hr 15 mins

1 Cook the carrot, cauliflower, broccoli, fennel and beans in a large saucepan of boiling water for 10 minutes until just tender. Drain the vegetables thoroughly and reserve.

2 Melt the butter in a saucepan over a low heat. Stir in the flour and cook for 1 minute. Remove from the heat and stir in the stock, wine and milk. Return to the heat and bring to the boil, stirring until thickened. Stir in the reserved vegetables, mushrooms and sage.

3 Meanwhile, make the topping. Cook the potatoes in a saucepan of boiling water for 10–15 minutes. Drain thoroughly and mash with the butter, yogurt and half the Parmesan cheese. Stir in the fennel seeds. Season to taste with salt and pepper.

4 Spoon the vegetable mixture into a 1-litre/1³/₄-pint pie dish. Spoon the potato over the top and sprinkle with the remaining cheese. Cook in a preheated oven, 190°C/375°F/Gas Mark 5, for 30–35 minutes or until golden. Serve the potato-topped vegetables hot.

This soufflé is very simple to make, yet it has a delicious flavour and melts in the mouth. Choose three alternative cheeses, if preferred.

Three Cheese Soufflé

1 Grease a 2.2-litre/4-pint soufflé dish and dust with the flour. Reserve.

2 Cook the potatoes in a saucepan of boiling water until tender. Mash until very smooth and then transfer to a mixing bowl to cool.

3 Beat the egg yolks into the potato and stir in the Gruyère cheese, blue cheese and Cheddar cheese. Mix, then season to taste with salt and pepper.

4 Whisk the egg whites in a clean bowl until standing in peaks, then gently fold them into the potato mixture with a metal spoon until incorporated.

5 Spoon the potato mixture into the prepared soufflé dish.

6 Cook in a preheated oven, 220°C/425°F/Gas Mark 7, for 35–40 minutes until risen and set. Serve the soufflé immediately.

SERVES 4

25 g/1 oz butter, for greasing
2 tsp plain flour, for dusting
900 g/2 lb floury potatoes
8 eggs, separated
25 g/1 oz Gruyère cheese, grated
25 g/1 oz blue cheese, crumbled
25 g/1 oz mature Cheddar cheese, grated
salt and pepper

NUTRITION
Calories *447*; Sugars *1 g*; Protein *22 g*;
Carbohydrate *41 g*; Fat *23 g*; Saturates *11 g*

easy

10 mins

55 mins

 COOK'S TIP

Insert a fine skewer into the centre of the soufflé – it should come out clean when the soufflé is fully cooked through.

128

This attractive and nutritious loaf is also utterly delicious. Served with a fresh tomato sauce, it can be eaten hot or cold with salad.

Nutty Harvest Loaf

SERVES 4

25 g/1 oz butter, plus extra for greasing
450 g/1 lb floury potatoes, diced
1 onion, chopped
2 garlic cloves, crushed
125 g/4½ oz unsalted peanuts
75 g/2¾ oz fresh white breadcrumbs
1 egg, beaten
2 tbsp chopped fresh coriander
150 ml/5 fl oz vegetable stock
75 g/2¾ oz sliced mushrooms
50 g/1¾ oz sun-dried tomatoes, sliced
salt and pepper
mixed salad leaves, to serve

sauce

150 ml/5 fl oz crème fraîche
2 tsp tomato purée
2 tsp clear honey
2 tbsp chopped fresh coriander

NUTRITION

Calories 554; Sugars 12 g; Protein 16 g;
Carbohydrate 43 g; Fat 37 g; Saturates 16 g

 moderate

20 mins

1 hr 20 mins

1 Grease a 450-g/1-lb loaf tin with butter. Cook the potatoes in a saucepan of boiling water for 10 minutes until cooked through. Drain, mash and reserve.

2 Melt half of the butter in a frying pan over a low heat. Add the onion and garlic and fry gently for 2–3 minutes until softened. Finely chop the nuts or process them in a food processor for 30 seconds with the breadcrumbs.

3 Mix the chopped nuts and breadcrumbs into the potatoes with the egg, coriander and vegetable stock. Stir in the onion and garlic and mix well.

4 Melt the remaining butter in the frying pan over a low heat. Add the sliced mushrooms and cook for 2–3 minutes.

5 Press half of the potato mixture into the base of the prepared loaf tin. Spoon the mushrooms on top and sprinkle with the sun-dried tomatoes. Spoon the remaining potato mixture on top and smooth the surface. Cover with foil and bake in a preheated oven, 190°C/375°F/Gas Mark 5, for 1 hour or until firm to the touch.

6 Meanwhile, mix the sauce ingredients together. Cut the nutty harvest loaf into slices and serve with the sauce.

COOK'S TIP

If you prefer, use unsalted cashew nuts instead of the peanuts.

This is a savoury version of a cheesecake with a layer of fried potatoes as a delicious base. Use frozen mixed vegetables for the topping, if you wish.

Vegetable Cake

1 Brush a 20-cm/8-inch springform cake tin with vegetable oil.

2 To make the base, heat the vegetable oil in a frying pan over a medium heat. Add the potato slices and cook until softened and browned. Drain on kitchen paper and arrange them neatly in the base of the tin.

3 To make the topping, heat the vegetable oil in a separate frying pan over a low heat. Add the leek and cook, stirring frequently, for about 3–4 minutes until softened.

4 Add the courgette, peppers, carrot and parsley to the pan and cook over a low heat for 5–7 minutes or until the vegetables have softened.

5 Meanwhile, beat the cheeses and eggs together in a bowl. Stir in the vegetables and season to taste with salt and pepper. Spoon the mixture evenly over the potato base.

6 Cook in a preheated oven, 190°C/375°F/Gas Mark 5, for 20–25 minutes until the vegetable cake is set.

7 Remove the vegetable cake from the tin, transfer to a warmed serving plate, garnish with shredded leek and serve with a crisp salad.

SERVES 4

base
2 tbsp vegetable oil, plus extra for brushing
1.25 kg/2 lb 12 oz waxy potatoes, sliced thinly

topping
1 tbsp vegetable oil
1 leek, chopped
1 courgette, grated
1 red pepper, deseeded and diced
1 green pepper, deseeded and diced
1 carrot, grated
2 tsp chopped fresh parsley
225 g/8 oz full-fat soft cheese
25 g/1 oz mature cheese, grated
2 eggs, beaten
salt and pepper
shredded cooked leek, to garnish
crisp salad, to serve

NUTRITION
Calories *502*; Sugars *8 g*; Protein *16 g*;
Carbohydrate *41 g*; Fat *31 g*; Saturates *14 g*

easy

20 mins

45 mins

This is an easy, but very filling meal. The potatoes are baked until fluffy, then they are mixed with a tasty pesto filling and baked again.

Twice-baked Pesto Potatoes

SERVES 4

4 baking potatoes
150 ml/5 fl oz double cream
5 tbsp vegetable stock
1 tbsp lemon juice
2 garlic cloves, crushed
3 tbsp chopped fresh basil
2 tbsp pine kernels
35 g/1¼ oz freshly grated Parmesan cheese
salt and pepper

1 Scrub the potatoes well and prick the skins with a fork. Rub a little salt into the skins and place on a baking tray.

2 Cook in a preheated oven, 190°C/375°F/Gas Mark 5, for 1 hour or until the potatoes are cooked through and the skins are crisp.

3 Remove the potatoes from the oven and cut them in half lengthways. Using a spoon, scoop the potato flesh into a mixing bowl, leaving a thin shell of potato inside the skins. Mash the potato flesh with a fork.

4 Meanwhile, mix the cream and vegetable stock together in a saucepan and simmer over a low heat for about 8–10 minutes or until reduced by half.

5 Stir in the lemon juice, garlic and chopped basil and season to taste with salt and pepper. Stir the mixture into the mashed potato flesh, together with the pine kernels.

6 Spoon the mixture back into the potato shells and sprinkle the Parmesan cheese on top. Return the potatoes to the oven for 10 minutes or until the cheese has browned. Serve hot.

NUTRITION
Calories *444*; Sugars *3 g*; Protein *10 g*;
Carbohydrate *40 g*; Fat *28 g*; Saturates *13 g*

⭐⭐   easy
🍳   10 mins
🕐   1 hr 20 mins

 COOK'S TIP

Add full-fat soft cheese or thinly sliced mushrooms to the mashed potato flesh at Step 5, if you prefer.

This tasty meal is made with sliced potatoes, tofu and vegetables, then topped with cheese and cooked in the pan from which it is served.

Pan Potato Cake

1 Cook the sliced potatoes in a large saucepan of boiling water for 10 minutes. Drain thoroughly.

2 Meanwhile, cook the carrot and broccoli florets in a separate saucepan of boiling water for 5 minutes. Drain with a slotted spoon.

3 Heat the butter and vegetable oil in a 23-cm/9-inch frying pan over a low heat. Add the onion and garlic and fry for 2–3 minutes. Add half of the potato slices to the frying pan, covering the base of the pan.

4 Cover the potato slices with the carrot, broccoli and the tofu. Sprinkle with half of the sage and cover with the remaining potato slices. Sprinkle the grated cheese over the top.

5 Cook over a medium heat for 8–10 minutes. Place the pan under a preheated medium–hot grill and cook for 2–3 minutes or until the cheese melts.

6 Garnish with the remaining sage and serve, straight from the pan.

SERVES 4

675 g/1 lb 8 oz waxy potatoes, unpeeled and sliced
1 carrot, diced
225 g/8 oz small broccoli florets
70 g/2½ oz butter
2 tbsp vegetable oil
1 red onion, quartered
2 garlic cloves, crushed
175 g/6 oz tofu, drained and diced
2 tbsp chopped fresh sage
75 g/2¾ oz mature Cheddar cheese, grated

NUTRITION
Calories *452*; Sugars *6 g*; Protein *17 g*;
Carbohydrate *35 g*; Fat *28 g*; Saturates *13 g*

  easy

🕐 15 mins

🕐 20 mins

🍽 **COOK'S TIP**

Make sure that the mixture fills the whole width of your frying pan to enable the layers to remain intact.

This is a quick dish to prepare and it can be left to cook in the oven without requiring any further attention.

Cheese *and* Potato Layer Bake

SERVES 4

900 g/2 lb waxy potatoes, unpeeled and cut into wedges
25 g/1 oz butter
1 red onion, halved and sliced
2 garlic cloves, crushed
2½ tbsp plain flour
600 ml/1 pint milk
400 g/14 oz canned artichoke hearts in brine, drained and halved
150 g/5½ oz frozen mixed vegetables, thawed
125 g/4½ oz Gruyère cheese, grated
125 g/4½ oz mature Cheddar cheese, grated
50 g/1¾ oz Gorgonzola cheese, crumbled
25 g/1 oz freshly grated Parmesan cheese
225 g/8 oz tofu, drained and sliced
2 tbsp chopped fresh thyme
salt and pepper
fresh thyme sprigs, to garnish

1 Parboil the potato wedges in a saucepan of boiling water for 10 minutes. Drain thoroughly and reserve.

2 Meanwhile, melt the butter in a saucepan over a low heat. Add the sliced onion and garlic and fry, stirring frequently, for 2–3 minutes.

3 Stir the flour into the pan and cook for 1 minute. Gradually add the milk, then increase the heat and bring to the boil, stirring constantly.

4 Reduce the heat and add the artichoke hearts, mixed vegetables, half of each of the 4 cheeses and all the tofu to the pan, mixing well. Stir in the chopped thyme and season to taste with salt and pepper.

5 Arrange a layer of potato wedges in the base of a shallow ovenproof dish. Spoon the vegetable mixture over the top and cover with the remaining potato wedges. Sprinkle the rest of the 4 cheeses over the top.

6 Cook in a preheated oven, 200°C/400°F/Gas Mark 6, for 30 minutes or until the potatoes are cooked and the top is golden-brown. Garnish the bake with a few sprigs of fresh thyme and serve immediately.

NUTRITION
Calories *766*; Sugars *14 g*; Protein *44 g*; Carbohydrate *60 g*; Fat *40 g*; Saturates *23 g*

easy

25 mins

45 mins

Similar to a simple moussaka, this recipe is made up of layers of aubergine, tomato and potato baked with a natural yogurt topping.

Potato *and* Aubergine Gratin

1 Cook the sliced potatoes in a saucepan of boiling water for 10 minutes until tender, but not breaking up. Drain and reserve.

2 Heat the vegetable oil in a frying pan over a low heat. Add the onion and garlic and fry, stirring occasionally, for 2–3 minutes.

3 Add the tofu, tomato purée and flour and cook for 1 minute. Gradually stir in the vegetable stock and bring to the boil, stirring. Reduce the heat and simmer for 10 minutes.

4 Arrange a layer of the potato slices in the base of a deep ovenproof dish. Spoon the tofu mixture evenly on top. Layer the sliced tomatoes, then the aubergine, and finally, the remaining potato slices on top of the tofu mixture, making sure that it is completely covered. Sprinkle with thyme.

5 Mix the yogurt and beaten eggs together in a bowl and season to taste with salt and pepper. Spoon the yogurt topping over the sliced potatoes to cover.

6 Bake in a preheated oven, 190°C/375°F/Gas Mark 5, for about 35–45 minutes or until the topping is browned. Serve.

SERVES 4

500 g/1 lb 2 oz waxy potatoes, sliced
1 tbsp vegetable oil
1 onion, chopped
2 garlic cloves, crushed
500 g/1 lb 2 oz tofu, drained and diced
2 tbsp tomato purée
2 tbsp plain flour
300 ml/10 fl oz vegetable stock
2 large tomatoes, sliced
1 aubergine, sliced
2 tbsp chopped fresh thyme
450 ml/16 fl oz natural yogurt
2 eggs, beaten
salt and pepper

NUTRITION
Calories *409*; Sugars *17 g*; Protein *28 g*;
Carbohydrate *45 g*; Fat *14 g*; Saturates *3 g*

 moderate

25 mins

 1 hr 15 mins

 COOK'S TIP

You can use marinated or smoked tofu for extra flavour, if you wish.

This delicious baked terrine has a base of mashed potato flavoured with nuts, cheese, herbs and spices.

Spicy Potato *and* Nut Terrine

SERVES 4

2 tbsp butter, plus extra for greasing
225 g/8 oz floury potatoes, diced
225 g/8 oz pecan nuts
225 g/8 oz unsalted cashew nuts
1 onion, chopped finely
2 garlic cloves, crushed
125 g/4½ oz open-cap mushrooms, diced
2 tbsp chopped mixed herbs
1 tsp paprika
1 tsp ground cumin
1 tsp ground coriander
4 eggs, beaten
125 g/4½ oz full-fat soft cheese
55 g/2 oz freshly grated Parmesan cheese
salt and pepper

sauce

3 large tomatoes, peeled, deseeded and
  chopped
2 tbsp tomato purée
5 tbsp red wine
1 tbsp red wine vinegar
pinch of caster sugar

NUTRITION

Calories *1100*; Sugars *13 g*; Protein *34 g*;
Carbohydrate *31 g*; Fat *93 g*; Saturates *22 g*

moderate

15 mins

1 hr 20 mins

1 Lightly grease a 900-g/2-lb loaf tin with butter and line with baking paper.

2 Cook the potatoes in a large saucepan of lightly salted boiling water for about 10 minutes or until cooked through. Drain thoroughly and mash.

3 Finely chop the pecan and cashew nuts or process in a food processor. Mix the nuts with the onion, garlic and mushrooms. Melt the butter in a frying pan over a low heat. Add the nut mixture and cook for 5–7 minutes. Add the herbs and spices. Stir in the eggs, cheeses and potatoes and season to taste with salt and pepper.

4 Spoon the mixture into the prepared loaf tin, pressing it down quite firmly. Cook in a preheated oven, 190°C/375°F/Gas Mark 5, for 1 hour or until set.

5 To make the sauce, mix the tomatoes, tomato purée, wine, wine vinegar and sugar in a pan and bring to the boil, stirring. Cook for 10 minutes or until the tomatoes have reduced. Rub the sauce through a sieve or process in a food processor for 30 seconds. Turn the terrine out of the tin on to a serving plate and cut into slices. Serve with the tomato sauce.

A wonderful mixture of red lentils, tofu and vegetables is cooked beneath a crunchy potato topping for a really hearty meal.

Potato-topped Lentil Bake

1 To make the topping, cook the potatoes in a saucepan of boiling water for 10 minutes or until cooked through. Drain well, add the butter and milk and mash thoroughly. Stir in the pecan nuts and chopped thyme and reserve.

2 Cook the lentils in boiling water for 20–30 minutes or until tender. Drain thoroughly and reserve.

3 Melt the butter in a frying pan over a medium heat. Add the leek, garlic, celery and broccoli and fry, stirring frequently, for 5 minutes until softened. Add the tofu cubes. Stir in the lentils, together with the tomato purée. Season to taste with salt and pepper, then transfer the mixture to the base of a shallow ovenproof dish.

4 Spoon the mashed potato evenly on top of the lentil mixture.

5 Cook in a preheated oven, 200°C/400°F/Gas Mark 6, for 30–35 minutes or until the topping is golden. Garnish the bake with sprigs of fresh thyme and serve hot.

SERVES 4

topping
675 g/1 lb 8 oz floury potatoes, diced
25 g/1 oz butter
1 tbsp milk
50 g/1³/₄ oz pecan nuts, chopped
2 tbsp chopped fresh thyme
fresh thyme sprigs, to garnish

filling
225 g/8 oz red lentils
70 g/2¹/₂ oz butter
1 leek, sliced
2 garlic cloves, crushed
1 celery stick, chopped
125 g/4¹/₂ oz broccoli florets
175 g/6 oz smoked tofu, drained and cubed
2 tsp tomato purée
salt and pepper

NUTRITION
Calories *627*; Sugars *7 g*; Protein *26 g*;
Carbohydrate *66 g*; Fat *30 g*; Saturates *13 g*

⭐⭐⭐ moderate
🕐 10 mins
🕐 1 hr 30 mins

🧑‍🍳 **COOK'S TIP**

You can use almost any combination of your favourite vegetables in this dish.

These strudels look really impressive and are perfect if friends are coming round. They are also suitable for a more formal dinner party dish.

Vegetable *and* Tofu Strudels

SERVES 4

filling
2 tbsp vegetable oil
25 g/1 oz butter
150 g/5½ oz potatoes, diced finely
1 leek, shredded
2 garlic cloves, crushed
1 tsp garam masala
½ tsp chilli powder
½ tsp turmeric
50 g/1¾ oz okra, sliced
100 g/3½ oz button mushrooms, sliced
2 tomatoes, diced
225 g/8 oz firm tofu, drained and diced
salt and pepper

pastry cases
350 g/12 oz (12 sheets) filo pastry
25 g/1 oz butter, melted
1 tbsp butter, for greasing

1 To make the filling, heat the vegetable oil and butter in a frying pan over a medium heat. Add the potatoes and leek and fry, stirring constantly, for about 2–3 minutes. Add the garlic and spices, okra, mushrooms, tomatoes, and tofu and season to taste with salt and pepper. Cook, stirring, for about 5–7 minutes or until tender.

2 Lay the pastry out on a chopping board and brush each individual sheet with melted butter. Place 3 sheets on top of one another. Repeat the process to make 4 stacks.

3 Spoon one-quarter of the filling along the centre of each stack and brush the edges with melted butter. Fold the short edges in and roll up lengthways to form a cigar shape. Brush the outside with melted butter. Place the strudels on a greased baking tray.

4 Cook in a preheated oven, 190°C/375°F/Gas Mark 5, for 20 minutes or until golden-brown and crisp. Transfer the strudels to a warmed serving dish and serve immediately.

NUTRITION
Calories *485*; Sugars *5 g*; Protein *16 g*;
Carbohydrate *47 g*; Fat *27 g*; Saturates *5 g*

✪✪✪   moderate

25 mins

30 mins

In this recipe, a variety of vegetables are cooked under a layer of potatoes, topped with cheese and then cooked until golden-brown.

Vegetable Hotpot

1 Cook the potato slices in a saucepan of boiling water for 10 minutes. Drain thoroughly and reserve.

2 Heat the vegetable oil in a flameproof casserole over a medium heat. Add the onion, leek and garlic and sauté, stirring occasionally, for 2–3 minutes. Add the remaining vegetables and cook, stirring, for a further 3–4 minutes.

3 Stir in the flour and cook for 1 minute. Gradually add the stock and cider and bring to the boil. Add the apple, sage and cayenne pepper and season well with salt and pepper. Remove from the heat and transfer the vegetables to an ovenproof dish.

4 Arrange the potato slices on top of the vegetable mixture to cover.

5 Sprinkle the cheese on top of the potato slices and cook in a preheated oven, 190°C/375°F/Gas Mark 5, for 30–35 minutes or until the potato is golden-brown and beginning to go crisp around the edges. Serve immediately.

SERVES 4

600 g/1 lb 5 oz potatoes, sliced thinly
2 tbsp vegetable oil
1 red onion, halved and sliced
1 leek, sliced
2 garlic cloves, crushed
1 carrot, cut into chunks
100 g/3½ oz broccoli florets
100 g/3½ oz cauliflower florets
2 small turnips, quartered
1 tbsp plain flour
700 ml/1¼ pints vegetable stock
150 ml/5 fl oz dry cider
1 eating apple, cored and sliced
2 tbsp chopped fresh sage
pinch of cayenne pepper
50 g/1¾ oz Cheddar cheese, grated
salt and pepper

NUTRITION
Calories *279*; Sugars *12 g*; Protein *10 g*; Carbohydrate *34 g*; Fat *11 g*; Saturates *4 g*

 easy

25 mins

1 hr

 COOK'S TIP

Vary the vegetables according to taste and availability. Gruyère cheese can replace the Cheddar cheese, if preferred.

Fish Dishes

There is no denying that fish and potatoes are a terrific combination. In these recipes potatoes are used in a variety of ways to enhance the fish. They are used to form a crispy coating for cod, and mashed to make the basis of fish cakes and fritters. They are sliced to form part of a layered pie, and sautéed with shallots to create the perfect accompaniment to a red mullet wrapped in Parma ham. These recipes also include some interesting flavours from France, such as Cotriade, a satisfying stew of fish and vegetables flavoured with herbs. For all health-conscious cooks, the nutritious value of these dishes is unbeatable.

This simple dish has a spicy breadcrumb topping over layers of cod and potatoes. It is cooked in the oven until crisp and golden.

Potato-topped Cod

SERVES 4

70 g/2½ oz butter
900 g/2 lb waxy potatoes, sliced
1 large onion, chopped finely
1 tsp wholegrain mustard
1 tsp garam masala
pinch of chilli powder
1 tbsp chopped fresh dill
75 g/2¾ oz fresh breadcrumbs
700 g/1 lb 9 oz cod fillet
50 g/1¾ oz Gruyère cheese, grated
salt and pepper
fresh dill sprigs, to garnish

1 Melt half of the butter in a frying pan over a low heat. Add the potatoes and fry for 5 minutes, turning until they are browned all over. Remove the potatoes from the pan with a slotted spoon.

2 Add the remaining butter to the frying pan and stir in the onion, mustard, garam masala, chilli powder, dill and breadcrumbs. Cook for 1–2 minutes, stirring and mixing well.

3 Layer half of the potatoes in the base of an ovenproof dish and place the cod fillets on top. Cover the cod fillets with the rest of the potato slices. Season to taste with salt and pepper.

4 Spoon the spicy mixture from the frying pan over the potato and sprinkle with the grated Gruyère cheese.

5 Cook in a preheated oven, 200°C/400°F/Gas Mark 6, for 20–25 minutes or until the topping is golden and crisp and the fish is cooked through. Remove from the oven, garnish with fresh dill sprigs and serve immediately.

NUTRITION
Calories 118; Sugars 1 g; Protein 10 g;
Carbohydrate 10 g; Fat 4.4 g; Saturates 2.6 g

⭐⭐⭐   moderate
🕐   5–10 mins
🕐   35 mins

👨‍🍳 **COOK'S TIP**

This dish is ideal served with baked vegetables, which can be cooked in the oven at the same time.

The base for this quiche is made with mashed potato instead of pastry, giving a softer textured case for the tasty tuna filling.

Tuna *and* Cheese Quiche

1 Cook the potatoes in a saucepan of boiling water for 10 minutes or until tender. Drain and mash. Add the butter and flour and mix to form a dough.

2 Knead the potato dough on a floured work surface and press the mixture into a 20-cm/8-inch flan tin. Prick the base with a fork. Line with baking paper and baking beans and bake the potato base blind in a preheated oven, 200°C/400°F/Gas Mark 6, for 20 minutes.

3 Heat the vegetable oil in a frying pan over a low heat. Add the shallot, garlic and pepper and fry gently for 5 minutes. Drain well and spoon the mixture into the prepared flan case. Flake the tuna and arrange it over the top with the sweetcorn.

4 Mix the milk, eggs and chopped dill together in a bowl. Season to taste with salt and pepper.

5 Pour the egg and dill mixture into the flan case and sprinkle the grated cheese evenly over the top.

6 Bake in the oven for 20 minutes or until the filling has set. Garnish with fresh dill and lemon wedges. Serve with mixed vegetables or salad.

SERVES 4

450 g/1 lb floury potatoes, diced
25 g/1 oz butter
6 tbsp plain flour, plus extra for dusting
mixed vegetables or salad, to serve

filling

1 tbsp vegetable oil
1 shallot, chopped
1 garlic clove, crushed
1 red pepper, diced
175 g/6 oz canned tuna in brine, drained
50 g/1¾ oz canned sweetcorn, drained
150 ml/5 fl oz skimmed milk
3 eggs, beaten
1 tbsp chopped fresh dill
50 g/1¾ oz mature low-fat Cheddar cheese, grated
salt and pepper

to garnish

fresh dill sprigs
lemon wedges

NUTRITION

Calories *383*; Sugars *5 g*; Protein *25 g*; Carbohydrate *40 g*; Fat *15 g*; Saturates *6 g*

 challenging

 20 mins

🕐 1 hr

This flavoursome and colourful fish pie is perfect for a light supper. The addition of smoked salmon gives it a touch of luxury.

Fish *and* Potato Pie

SERVES 4

900 g/2 lb smoked haddock or cod fillets
600 ml/1 pint skimmed milk
2 bay leaves
115 g/4 oz button mushrooms, quartered
115 g/4 oz frozen peas
115 g/4 oz frozen sweetcorn
675 g/1 lb 8 oz potatoes, diced
5 tbsp low-fat natural yogurt
4 tbsp chopped fresh parsley
55 g/2 oz smoked salmon, sliced into thin strips
3 tbsp cornflour
25 g/1 oz smoked cheese, grated
salt and pepper

NUTRITION
Calories *523*; Sugars *15 g*; Protein *58 g*;
Carbohydrate *63 g*; Fat *6 g*; Saturates *2 g*

easy

15 mins

1 hr

1 Place the fish in a saucepan and add the milk and bay leaves. Bring to the boil, cover and simmer for 5 minutes.

2 Add the mushrooms, peas and sweetcorn, bring back to a simmer, cover and cook for 5–7 minutes. Leave to cool.

3 Cook the potatoes in a large saucepan of boiling water for 8 minutes. Drain well and mash. Stir in the yogurt, parsley and seasoning. Reserve.

4 Using a slotted spoon, remove the fish from the pan. Carefully flake the fish away from the skin and place in a large ovenproof gratin dish. Reserve the cooking liquid.

5 Drain the vegetables, reserving the cooking liquid, and gently stir into the fish with the salmon strips.

6 Blend a little cooking liquid into the cornflour to make a paste. Transfer the rest of the liquid to a saucepan and add the paste. Heat through, stirring until thickened. Remove and discard the bay leaves and season to taste with salt and pepper. Pour the sauce over the fish and vegetables and mix. Cover the fish with the mashed potato, sprinkle with cheese and bake in a preheated oven, 200°C/400°F/Gas Mark 6, for 25–30 minutes.

COOK'S TIP

For a milder flavour, use unsmoked cod or haddock fillet and replace the parsley with dill.

Mediterranean cooks have always made the most of dried salted cod, once the only source of cod during harsh winter months.

Salt Cod Fritters

1 Break the salt cod into pieces and place in a bowl. Add enough water to cover and leave for 48 hours, changing the water 4 times.

2 Drain the salt cod, then cook in boiling water for 20–25 minutes until tender. Drain, then remove all the skin and bones. Using a fork, flake the fish into fine pieces that still retain some texture.

3 Meanwhile, cook the potatoes in their skins in a saucepan of boiling water until tender. Drain, peel and mash in a large bowl. Reserve.

4 Heat 1 tablespoon of the olive oil in a frying pan over a low heat. Add the onion and garlic and fry for 5 minutes, stirring until softened, but not brown. Remove with a slotted spoon and drain on kitchen paper.

5 Stir the salt cod, onion and garlic into the mashed potatoes. Stir in the parsley and capers (if using). Season generously with pepper.

6 Stir in the beaten egg. Cover the salt cod mixture and leave to chill for 30 minutes, then adjust the seasoning, if necessary.

7 Heat 5 cm/2 inches of oil in a deep saucepan to 180°–190°C/350–375°F, or until a cube of bread browns in 30 seconds. Drop tablespoonfuls of the salt-cod mixture into the hot oil and fry for about 8 minutes or until golden-brown and set. Do not fry more than 6 at a time because the oil will become too cold and the fritters will become soggy. You will get 18–20 fritters. Drain on kitchen paper. Transfer to a large serving plate, garnish with parsley and serve with aïoli for dipping.

SERVES 4

450 g/1 lb salt cod
350 g/12 oz floury baking potatoes
1 tbsp olive oil, plus extra for deep-frying
1 onion, chopped very finely
1 garlic clove, crushed
4 tbsp very finely chopped fresh parsley or coriander
1 tbsp capers in brine, drained and finely chopped (optional)
1 small egg, beaten lightly
salt and pepper
fresh flat-leaved parsley sprigs, to garnish
aïoli, to serve

NUTRITION
Calories *300*; Sugars *1 g*; Protein *16 g*; Carbohydrate *11 g*; Fat *22 g*; Saturates *3 g*

⭐⭐⭐   moderate

🌀   48 hrs 30 mins

     45 mins

This is a rich French stew of fish and vegetables, flavoured with saffron and herbs. The fish and vegetables, and the soup, are served separately.

Cotriade

SERVES 6

large pinch of saffron
600 ml/1 pint hot fish stock
1 tbsp olive oil
25 g/1 oz butter
1 onion, sliced
2 garlic cloves, chopped
1 leek, sliced
1 small fennel bulb, sliced finely
450 g/1 lb potatoes, cut into chunks
150 ml/5 fl oz dry white wine
1 tbsp fresh thyme leaves
2 bay leaves
4 ripe tomatoes, peeled and chopped
900 g/2 lb mixed fish such as haddock, hake, mackerel, red or grey mullet, chopped roughly
2 tbsp chopped fresh parsley
salt and pepper

to garnish
lemon slices
fresh dill sprigs

NUTRITION
Calories *81*; Sugars *1 g*; Protein *7 g*;
Carbohydrate *4 g*; Fat *4 g*; Saturates *1 g*

 moderate
 15 mins
15 mins
40 mins

1 Using a mortar and pestle, crush the saffron and add to the fish stock. Stir the mixture and leave to infuse for at least 10 minutes.

2 Heat the olive oil and butter together over a low heat in a large saucepan. Add the onion and cook gently for 4–5 minutes until softened. Add the garlic, leek, fennel and potatoes. Cover and cook for a further 10–15 minutes until the vegetables are softened.

3 Add the wine and simmer rapidly for 3–4 minutes until reduced by half. Add the thyme, bay leaves and tomatoes and stir well. Add the saffron-infused fish stock. Bring to the boil, cover and simmer gently for 15 minutes until the vegetables are tender.

4 Add the fish, return to the boil and simmer for a further 3–4 minutes until all the fish is tender. Add the parsley and season to taste with salt and pepper. Using a slotted spoon, remove the fish and vegetables to a warmed serving dish and garnish with a few sprigs of fresh dill and lemon slices. Serve immediately.

COOK'S TIP

Once the fish and vegetables have been cooked, you could process the soup and rub it through a sieve to give a smooth fish soup.

Try to get small red mullet for this dish. If you can only get larger fish, serve one to each person and increase the cooking time accordingly.

Grilled Red Mullet

1 For the sauté potatoes and shallots, heat the olive oil in a large frying pan over a low heat. Add the potatoes, garlic and shallots. Cook gently, stirring regularly, for 12–15 minutes until they are golden, crisp and tender.

2 Meanwhile, divide the lemon slices, halved if necessary, garlic, parsley, thyme, sage and shallots between the cavities of the fish. Season well with salt and pepper. Wrap a slice of Parma ham around each fish. Secure with a cocktail stick.

3 Arrange the fish on a grill pan and cook under a preheated hot grill for about 5–6 minutes on each side until tender.

4 To make the dressing, mix the olive oil, lemon juice, chopped parsley and chives together. Season to taste with salt and pepper.

5 Divide the potatoes and shallots between 4 large serving plates and top each with the fish. Drizzle around the dressing and serve immediately with salad leaves.

SERVES 4

1 lemon, sliced thinly
2 garlic cloves, crushed
4 fresh flat-leaved parsley sprigs
4 fresh thyme sprigs
8 fresh sage leaves
2 large shallots, sliced
8 small red mullet, cleaned
8 slices Parma ham
salt and pepper
salad leaves, to serve

sauté potatoes and shallots
4 tbsp olive oil
900 g/2 lb potatoes, diced
8 whole garlic cloves, unpeeled
12 small whole shallots

dressing
4 tbsp olive oil
1 tbsp lemon juice
1 tbsp chopped fresh flat-leaved parsley
1 tbsp snipped fresh chives

NUTRITION
Calories *111*; Sugars *1 g*; Protein *10 g*; Carbohydrate *6 g*; Fat *5 g*; Saturates *0.7 g*

 moderate

 10 mins

20 mins

POTATOES

This colourful dish is served cold, and therefore makes a lovely summer lunch or supper dish.

Poached Rainbow Trout

SERVES 4

1.3 kg/3 lb rainbow trout fillet, cleaned
700 g/1 lb 9 oz new potatoes
3 spring onions, chopped finely
1 egg, hard-boiled and chopped

court-bouillon
850 ml/1½ pints cold water
850 ml/1½ pints dry white wine
3 tbsp white wine vinegar
2 large carrots, chopped roughly
1 onion, chopped roughly
2 celery sticks, chopped roughly
2 leeks, chopped roughly
2 garlic cloves, chopped roughly
2 bay leaves
4 sprigs each of fresh parsley and thyme
6 black peppercorns
1 tsp salt

watercress mayonnaise
1 egg yolk
1 tsp each of Dijon mustard and wine vinegar
55 g/2 oz watercress leaves, chopped
225 ml/8 fl oz light olive oil
salt and pepper

NUTRITION

Calories *99*; Sugars *1 g*; Protein *6 g*;
Carbohydrate *4 g*; Fat *6 g*; Saturates *1 g*

★★★   moderate

🕐   25 mins

🕐   1 hr 5 mins

1 To make the court-bouillon, place all the ingredients in a large saucepan and bring slowly to the boil. Cover and simmer gently for about 30 minutes. Strain the liquid through a fine sieve into a clean pan. Bring to the boil again and simmer rapidly, uncovered, for 15–20 minutes until the court-bouillon is reduced to 600 ml/1 pint.

2 Place the trout in a large frying pan. Add the court-bouillon and bring slowly to the boil. Remove from the heat and cool the fish in the poaching liquid.

3 Meanwhile, make the watercress mayonnaise. Put the egg yolk, mustard, wine vinegar, watercress and seasoning into a food processor or blender and process for 30 seconds until foaming. Gradually add the olive oil, drop by drop, until the mixture begins to thicken. Continue adding the oil in a slow steady stream until all the oil is incorporated. Add a little hot water if the mixture seems too thick. Season to taste with salt and pepper and reserve.

4 Cook the potatoes in a saucepan of boiling salted water for 12–15 minutes until tender. Drain and refresh them under cold running water. Cool.

5 When the potatoes are cold, cut them in half if they are very large, and toss thoroughly with the watercress mayonnaise, the spring onions and egg.

6 Carefully lift the fish from the poaching liquid and drain on kitchen paper. Carefully pull the skin away from each of the trout and serve immediately with the potato salad.

This is a fish pie for pushing the boat out! Try piping the potato topping decoratively over the pie – it looks wonderful when baked.

Luxury Fish Pie

1 To make the filling, melt 25 g/1 oz of the butter in a frying pan over a high heat. Add the shallots and cook for 5 minutes until softened. Add the mushrooms and cook for 2 minutes. Add the wine and simmer until the liquid has evaporated. Transfer to a 1.5-litre/2³/₄-pint shallow ovenproof dish and reserve.

2 Put the mussels into a large saucepan with just the water that clings to their shells and cook, covered, over a high heat for 3–4 minutes until all the mussels have opened. Discard any that remain closed. Drain, reserving the cooking liquid. When cool enough to handle, remove the mussels from their shells and add to the mushrooms.

3 Bring the court-bouillon to a boil and add the monkfish. Poach for 2 minutes before adding the cod, sole and prawns. Poach for a further 2 minutes. Remove the fish with a slotted spoon and add to the mussels and mushrooms.

4 Melt the remaining butter in a saucepan and add the flour. Stir until smooth and cook for 2 minutes. Gradually, stir in the hot court-bouillon and mussel cooking liquid until thickened. Add the cream and simmer for 15 minutes, stirring. Season to taste with salt and pepper and pour over the fish.

5 Meanwhile, make the topping. Boil the potatoes in plenty of salted water for 15–20 minutes until tender. Drain and mash with the butter, egg yolks, milk, nutmeg and seasoning. Pipe over the fish and roughen with a fork.

6 Bake the pie in a preheated oven, 200°C/400° F/Gas Mark 6, for 30 minutes until golden. Garnish with parsley to serve.

SERVES 4

85 g/3 oz butter
3 shallots, chopped finely
115 g/4 oz button mushrooms, halved
2 tbsp dry white wine
900 g/2 lb live mussels, scrubbed and debearded
1 quantity court-bouillon (see page 146)
300 g/10¹/₂ oz monkfish fillet, cubed
300 g/10¹/₂ oz skinless cod fillet, cubed
300 g/10¹/₂ oz skinless lemon sole fillet, cubed
115 g/4 oz tiger prawns, peeled
2¹/₂ tbsp plain flour
3 tbsp double cream

potato topping
1.5 kg/3 lb 5 oz floury potatoes,
    cut into chunks
4 tbsp butter
2 egg yolks
125 ml/4 fl oz milk
pinch of freshly grated nutmeg
salt and pepper
fresh parsley sprigs, to garnish

NUTRITION
Calories *863*; Sugars *5 g*; Protein *66 g*;
Carbohydrate *60 g*; Fat *41 g*; Saturates *24 g*

 moderate

10 mins

1 hr 10 mins

Poultry *and* Meat

This chapter contains a wide selection of delicious main meal dishes. The potato is the main ingredient in the majority of these recipes, but there are also ideas for adding meat, poultry and vegetables, so that there is sure to be something for everyone. The recipes come from all around the world – try Potato Ravioli or Curried Stir-fried Lamb. There are also hearty dishes including Quick Chicken Bake, and Lamb Hotpot. Whatever the occasion, you are sure to find something here to entice you.

Potato cakes are a great favourite. In this recipe the potatoes are combined with minced chicken and mashed banana.

Chicken *and* Banana Cakes

SERVES 4

450 g/1 lb floury potatoes, diced
225 g/8 oz minced chicken
1 large banana
2 tbsp plain flour, plus extra for dusting
1 tsp lemon juice
1 onion, chopped finely
2 tbsp chopped fresh sage
25 g/1 oz butter
2 tbsp vegetable oil
150 ml/5 fl oz single cream
150 ml/5 fl oz chicken stock
salt and pepper
fresh sage leaves, to garnish

1 Cook the diced potatoes in a saucepan of boiling water for 10 minutes until cooked through. Drain and mash the potatoes until smooth. Stir in the minced chicken and mix thoroughly.

2 Mash the banana and add it to the potato with the flour, lemon juice, onion and half of the chopped sage. Season well with salt and pepper and stir the mixture together.

3 Divide the mixture equally into 8 portions. With lightly floured hands, shape each portion into a round patty.

4 Heat the butter and vegetable oil in a frying pan over a medium heat. Add the potato cakes and cook for 12–15 minutes or until cooked through, turning once. Remove from the pan and keep warm.

5 Stir the cream and stock into the pan with the remaining chopped sage. Cook over a low heat for 2–3 minutes.

6 Arrange the potato cakes on a serving plate, garnish with fresh sage leaves and serve with the cream and sage sauce.

NUTRITION

Calories *439*; Sugars *11 g*; Protein *22 g*;
Carbohydrate *39 g*; Fat *23 g*; Saturates *10 g*

★★★   moderate

🕐   5–10 mins

🕐   25–30 mins

 COOK'S TIP

Do not boil the sauce once the cream has been added or it will curdle. Cook it gently over a very low heat.

This is a layered pie of potatoes, broccoli, tomatoes and chicken slices in a creamy sauce, topped with a crisp oat layer.

Potato Crisp Pie

1 Cook the potatoes in a saucepan of boiling water for 10 minutes. Drain the potatoes thoroughly and reserve.

2 Meanwhile, melt the butter in a frying pan over a medium–low heat. Cut the chicken into strips and cook for 5 minutes, turning. Add the garlic and spring onions to the chicken and cook for a further 2 minutes.

3 Stir in the flour and cook for 1 minute. Gradually add the wine and cream. Bring to the boil, stirring, then reduce the heat until the sauce is simmering, then cook for 5 minutes.

4 Blanch the broccoli in a pan of boiling water, drain and refresh in cold water.

5 Place half of the potatoes in the base of a pie dish and top with half of the tomatoes and half of the broccoli.

6 Spoon the chicken sauce on top of the vegetables and repeat the layers in the same order once more.

7 Arrange the Gruyère cheese on top and spoon over the yogurt. Sprinkle with the oats and cook in a preheated oven, 200°C/400°F/Gas Mark 6, for 25 minutes until the top is golden-brown. Serve the pie immediately.

🎩 **COOK'S TIP**

Add chopped nuts, such as pine kernels, to the topping for extra crunch.

SERVES 4

600 g/1 lb 5 oz waxy potatoes, sliced
70 g/2½ oz butter
1 skinned chicken breast fillet, about 175 g/6 oz
2 garlic cloves, crushed
4 spring onions, sliced
2½ tbsp plain flour
150 ml/5 fl oz dry white wine
150 ml/5 fl oz double cream
225 g/8 oz broccoli florets
4 large tomatoes, sliced
85 g/3 oz Gruyère cheese, sliced
225 ml/8 fl oz natural yogurt
25 g/1 oz rolled oats, toasted

NUTRITION
Calories 630; Sugars 12 g; Protein 25 g; Carbohydrate 38 g; Fat 40 g; Saturates 24 g

⭐⭐   easy
   10 mins
   55 mins

This pie has an attractive filo pastry case that has a 'ruffled' top made with strips of the pastry brushed with melted butter.

Potato, Leek *and* Chicken Pie

SERVES 4

225 g/8 oz waxy potatoes, cubed
70 g/2½ oz butter
1 skinned chicken breast fillet, about
    175 g/6 oz, cubed
1 leek, sliced
150 g/5½ oz chestnut mushrooms, sliced
2½ tbsp plain flour
300 ml/10 fl oz milk
1 tbsp Dijon mustard
2 tbsp chopped fresh sage
225 g/8 oz filo pastry, thawed if frozen
3 tbsp butter, melted
salt and pepper

1 Cook the potato cubes in a saucepan of boiling water for 5 minutes. Drain thoroughly and reserve.

2 Melt the butter in a frying pan over a medium heat. Add the chicken cubes and cook for 5 minutes or until browned all over.

3 Add the leek and mushrooms and cook for 3 minutes, stirring. Stir in the flour and cook for 1 minute. Gradually add the milk and bring to the boil. Add the mustard, sage and potato cubes, then simmer for 10 minutes.

4 Meanwhile, line a deep pie dish with half of the sheets of filo pastry. Spoon the sauce into the dish and cover with one sheet of pastry. Brush the pastry with butter and lay another sheet on top. Brush this sheet with butter.

5 Cut the remaining filo pastry into strips and fold them on to the top of the pie to create a ruffled effect. Brush the strips with the melted butter and cook in a preheated oven 180°C/350°F/Gas Mark 4, for 45 minutes or until golden-brown and crisp. Serve hot.

NUTRITION
Calories 543; Sugars 7 g; Protein 21 g;
Carbohydrate 56 g; Fat 27 g; Saturates 16 g

★★★ moderate

🕐 10 mins

🕐 1 hr 15 mins

🍳 COOK'S TIP

If the top of the pie begins to brown too quickly, cover it with foil halfway through the cooking time to allow the pastry base to cook through without the top burning.

This recipe is a type of shepherd's pie and is just as versatile. Add vegetables and herbs of your choice, depending on what you have to hand.

Quick Chicken Bake

1 Brown the chicken mince, onion and carrots in a non-stick frying pan for about 5 minutes, stirring frequently.

2 Sprinkle the chicken with the flour and simmer for a further 2 minutes.

3 Gradually blend in the tomato purée and stock, then simmer for 15 minutes. Season to taste with salt and pepper and add the thyme.

4 Transfer mixture to an ovenproof casserole and leave to cool.

5 Spoon the mashed potato over the chicken mixture and sprinkle with cheese. Bake in a preheated oven at 200°C/400°F/Gas Mark 6, for about 20 minutes or until the cheese is bubbling and golden, then serve, straight from the casserole, with freshly cooked peas.

SERVES 4

500/1 lb 2 oz g chicken mince
1 large onion, chopped finely
2 carrots, chopped finely
2 tbsp plain flour
1 tbsp tomato purée
300 ml/10 fl oz chicken stock
pinch of fresh thyme
1.5 kg/3 lb 5 oz mashed potatoes, creamed
    with butter and milk and highly seasoned
75 g/2³/₄ oz grated cheese, such as Cheddar
salt and pepper
freshly cooked peas, to serve

NUTRITION
Calories *496*; Sugars *10 g*; Protein *38 g*;
Carbohydrate *52 g*; Fat *17 g*; Saturates *9 g*

  moderate

🕐 25 mins

🕐 45 mins

 COOK'S TIP

Instead of plain cheese, you could sprinkle a flavoured cheese over the top. There are a variety of cheeses blended with onion and chives, and these are ideal for melting as a topping.

There are many regional versions of hotpot, all using fresh, local ingredients available all year, perfect for traditional one-pot cooking.

Country Chicken Hotpot

SERVES 4

4 chicken quarters
6 medium potatoes, cut into 5-mm/¼-inch slices
2 fresh thyme sprigs
2 fresh rosemary sprigs
2 bay leaves
200 g/7 oz smoked bacon, rinded and diced
1 large onion, chopped finely
2 carrots, sliced
150 ml/5 fl oz stout
25 g/1 oz melted butter
salt and pepper
freshly cooked seasonal vegetables, to serve (optional)

1 Remove the skin from the chicken quarters, if wished.

2 Arrange a layer of potato slices in the base of a wide casserole. Season to taste with salt and pepper, then add the thyme, rosemary and bay leaves.

3 Top with the chicken quarters, then sprinkle with the diced bacon, onion, and carrots. Season well with salt and pepper and carefully arrange the remaining potato slices on top, overlapping them slightly.

4 Pour over the stout, brush the potatoes with the melted butter, and cover the casserole with a lid.

5 Bake in a preheated oven, 150°C/300°F/Gas Mark 2, for about 2 hours, uncovering the casserole for the last 30 minutes to let the potatoes brown. Serve hot with fresh seasonal vegetables, if wished.

NUTRITION
Calories *499*; Sugars *6 g*; Protein *43 g*;
Carbohydrate *44 g*; Fat *17 g*; Saturates *8 g*

⭐⭐⭐ moderate
 10 mins
 2 hrs

COOK'S TIP

This dish is also delicious with stewing lamb, cut into chunks. You can add different vegetables depending on what is in season – try leeks and swede for a slightly sweeter flavour.

Turkey is especially good with fruit, because it has a fairly strong flavour. The walnuts counteract the sweetness of the fruit.

Potato *and* Turkey Pie

1 Cook the diced potatoes in a saucepan of boiling water for 10 minutes until tender. Drain and reserve.

2 Meanwhile, heat the butter and oil in a saucepan over a medium heat. Add the turkey and cook for 5 minutes, turning until browned.

3 Add the sliced onion and cook for 2–3 minutes. Stir in the flour and cook for 1 minute. Gradually stir in the milk and the cream. Bring to the boil, stirring, then reduce the heat until the mixture is simmering.

4 Stir in the celery, apricots, walnut pieces, parsley and potatoes. Season well with salt and pepper. Spoon the potato and turkey mixture into the base of a 1.2-litre/2-pint pie dish.

5 Roll out the pastry on a lightly floured work surface until it is 2.5-cm/1-inch larger than the dish. Trim a 2.5-cm/1-inch wide strip from the pastry and place the strip on the dampened rim of the dish. Brush with water and cover with the pastry lid, pressing to seal the edges.

6 Brush the top of the pie with beaten egg and cook in a preheated oven, 200°C/400°F/Gas Mark 6, for 25–30 minutes or until the pastry is cooked and golden-brown. Serve immediately.

SERVES 4

300 g/10½ oz waxy potatoes, diced
25 g/1 oz butter
1 tbsp vegetable oil
300 g/10½ oz lean turkey meat, cubed
1 red onion, halved and sliced
2 tbsp plain flour, plus extra for dusting
300 ml/10 fl oz milk
150 ml/5 fl oz double cream
2 celery sticks, sliced
75 g/2¾ oz dried apricots, chopped
25 g/1 oz walnut pieces
2 tbsp chopped fresh parsley
salt and pepper
225 g/8 oz ready-made shortcrust pastry
beaten egg, for brushing

NUTRITION
Calories *790*; Sugars *16 g*; Protein *28 g*;
Carbohydrate *60 g*; Fat *50 g*; Saturates *23 g*

  challenging
10 mins
50 mins

In this recipe, the potatoes are cooked in the goulash. For a change, you may prefer to substitute small, scrubbed new potatoes.

Beef *and* Potato Goulash

S E R V E S 4

2 tbsp vegetable oil
1 large onion, sliced
2 garlic cloves, crushed
750 g/1 lb 10 oz lean stewing steak
2 tbsp paprika
400 g/14 oz canned chopped tomatoes
2 tbsp tomato purée
1 large red pepper, deseeded and chopped
175 g/6 oz mushrooms, wiped and sliced
600 ml/1 pint beef stock
500 g/1 lb 2 oz potatoes, cut into
    large chunks
1 tbsp cornflour
salt and pepper

to garnish
4 tbsp low-fat natural yogurt
paprika
chopped fresh parsley

N U T R I T I O N
Calories *477*; Sugars *11 g*; Protein *47 g*;
Carbohydrate *39 g*; Fat *16 g*; Saturates *5 g*

 challenging
15 mins
2 hrs 15 mins

1 Heat the vegetable oil in a large saucepan over a medium heat. Add the onion and garlic and fry for 3–4 minutes until softened.

2 Cut the steak into chunks and cook over a high heat for about 3 minutes until browned all over.

3 Add the paprika and stir well. Add the tomatoes, tomato purée, red pepper and mushrooms. Cook the vegetables for 2 minutes, stirring constantly.

4 Pour in the stock. Bring to the boil, then reduce the heat. Cover and simmer for about 1½ hours until the meat is tender.

5 Add the potatoes and cook, covered, for 20–30 minutes until tender.

6 Blend the cornflour with a little water to make a smooth paste and add to the saucepan, stirring until blended and thickened. Cook for 1 minute, then season to taste with salt and pepper. Top the goulash with the yogurt, sprinkle over the paprika, garnish with chopped fresh parsley and serve.

In this recipe the 'pasta' dough is made with potatoes instead of flour. The ravioli are filled with bolognese sauce and cooked in a frying pan.

Potato Ravioli

1   To make the bolognese filling, heat the vegetable oil in a frying pan over a medium heat. Add the beef and fry for 3–4 minutes, breaking it up with a wooden spoon. Add the shallot and garlic and cook for about 2–3 minutes until the shallot has softened.

2   Stir in the flour and tomato purée and cook for 1 minute. Stir in the beef stock, celery, tomatoes and basil. Season to taste with salt and pepper.

3   Cook the bolognese sauce over a low heat for 20 minutes. Remove the sauce from the heat and leave to cool.

4   To make the ravioli, cook the potatoes in a saucepan of boiling water for 10 minutes until cooked.

5   Mash the potatoes and place them in a mixing bowl. Blend in the egg yolks and olive oil. Season to taste with salt and pepper, then stir in the flour and mix to form a dough.

6   Divide the dough into 24 pieces on a lightly floured work surface and form into flat rounds. Spoon the filling on to one half of each round and fold the dough over to encase the filling, pressing down to seal the edges.

7   Melt the butter in a large frying pan over a medium heat. Add the ravioli, in batches, and cook for 6–8 minutes, turning once, until golden. Transfer to 4 serving plates, garnish with shredded basil and serve hot.

SERVES   4

filling
1 tbsp vegetable oil
125 g/4½ oz beef mince
1 shallot, diced
1 garlic clove, crushed
1 tbsp plain flour
1 tbsp tomato purée
150 ml/5 fl oz beef stock
1 celery stick, chopped
2 tomatoes, peeled and diced
2 tsp chopped fresh basil
salt and pepper

ravioli
450 g/1 lb floury potatoes, diced
3 small egg yolks
3 tbsp olive oil
175 g/6 oz plain flour, plus extra for dusting
70 g/2½ oz butter, for frying
shredded fresh basil leaves, to garnish

NUTRITION
Calories *559*; Sugars *4 g*; Protein *17 g*;
Carbohydrate *60 g*; Fat *30 g*; Saturates *11 g*

   moderate

   5–10 mins

   1 hr 10 mins

This dish is really superb if made with tender veal. However, if veal is unavailable, use pork or turkey escalopes instead.

Veal Italienne

SERVES 4

70 g/2½ oz butter
1 tbsp olive oil
675 g/1 lb 8 oz potatoes, cubed
4 veal escalopes, about 175 g/6 oz each
1 onion, cut into 8 wedges
2 garlic cloves, crushed
2 tbsp plain flour
2 tbsp tomato purée
150 ml/5 fl oz red wine
300 ml/10 fl oz chicken stock
8 ripe tomatoes, peeled, deseeded and diced
25 g/1 oz stoned black olives, halved
2 tbsp chopped fresh basil
salt and pepper
fresh basil leaves, to garnish

1 Heat the butter and olive oil in a large frying pan over a medium heat. Add the potato cubes and cook for 5–7 minutes, stirring frequently, until they begin to brown.

2 Remove the potatoes from the pan with a slotted spoon and reserve.

3 Place the veal in the frying pan and cook for 2–3 minutes on each side until sealed. Remove from the pan and reserve.

4 Stir the onion and garlic into the pan and cook for 2–3 minutes.

5 Add the flour and tomato purée and cook for 1 minute, stirring constantly. Gradually blend in the red wine and chicken stock, stirring to make a smooth sauce.

6 Return the potatoes and veal to the pan. Stir in the tomatoes, olives and basil and season to taste with salt and pepper.

7 Transfer to a casserole dish and cook in a preheated oven, 180°C/350°F/Gas Mark 4, for 1 hour or until the potatoes and veal are cooked through. Garnish with basil leaves and serve.

NUTRITION

Calories 592; Sugars 5 g; Protein 44 g;
Carbohydrate 48 g; Fat 23 g; Saturates 9 g

 moderate

 25 mins

1 hr 20 mins

COOK'S TIP

For a quicker cooking time and really tender meat, pound the meat with a meat mallet or rolling pin to flatten it slightly before cooking.

This classic recipe using lamb cutlets layered between sliced potatoes, kidneys, onions and herbs makes a perfect meal on a cold winter's day.

Lamb Hotpot

1 Remove any excess fat from the lamb. Skin and core the kidneys and cut them into slices. Reserve.

2 Arrange an even layer of sliced potatoes in the base of a 1.7-litre/3-pint oven-proof baking dish.

3 Arrange the lamb neck cutlets on top of the potatoes and cover with the sliced kidneys, onion and thyme.

4 Pour the lamb stock over the lamb neck cutlets and season to taste with salt and pepper.

5 Layer the remaining potato slices on top, overlapping to cover the meat and sliced onion completely.

6 Brush the potato slices with the melted butter, cover the dish and cook in a preheated oven, 180°C/350°F/Gas Mark 4, for 1½ hours.

7 Remove the lid and cook for a further 30 minutes until golden-brown on top.

8 Garnish with fresh thyme sprigs and serve hot.

SERVES 4

675 g/1 lb 8 oz lean lamb neck cutlets
2 lamb's kidneys
675 g/1 lb 8 oz waxy potatoes, scrubbed and thinly sliced
1 large onion, sliced thinly
2 tbsp chopped fresh thyme
150 ml/5 fl oz lamb stock
25 g/1 oz butter, melted
salt and pepper
fresh thyme sprigs, to garnish

NUTRITION
Calories *420*; Sugars *2 g*; Protein *41 g*;
Carbohydrate *31 g*; Fat *15 g*; Saturates *8 g*

⭐⭐ easy

🖐 15 mins

🕐 2 hrs

 COOK'S TIP

Traditionally, oysters are also included in this tasty hotpot. Add them to the layers along with the kidneys, if wished.

POTATOES

In this variation of a traditional Spanish dish, eggs are cooked on top of a spicy sausage, tomato and potato mixture.

Spanish Potato Bake

SERVES 4

675 g/1 lb 8 oz waxy potatoes, diced
3 tbsp olive oil
1 onion, halved and sliced
2 garlic cloves, crushed
400 g/14 oz canned plum tomatoes, chopped
75 g/2³⁄₄ oz chorizo sausage, sliced
1 green pepper, cut into strips
¹⁄₂ tsp paprika
25 g/1 oz stoned black olives, halved
8 eggs
1 tbsp chopped fresh parsley
salt and pepper
crusty bread, to serve (optional)

1 Cook the diced potatoes in a saucepan of boiling water for 10 minutes or until softened. Drain and reserve.

2 Heat the olive oil in a large frying pan over a low heat. Add the onion and garlic and fry gently for 2–3 minutes until the onion has softened.

3 Add the tomatoes and cook over a low heat for about 10 minutes until the mixture has reduced slightly.

4 Stir the potatoes into the pan with the chorizo, green pepper, paprika and olives. Season to taste with salt and pepper. Cook for 5 minutes, stirring. Transfer to a shallow ovenproof dish.

5 Make 8 small hollows in the top of the mixture and break an egg into each.

6 Cook in a preheated oven, 220°C/425°F/Gas Mark 7, for 5–6 minutes or until the eggs are just cooked. Sprinkle with chopped parsley and serve with crusty bread, if wished.

NUTRITION
Calories 443; Sugars 7 g; Protein 21 g; Carbohydrate 36 g; Fat 25 g; Saturates 8 g

easy

5 mins

35 mins

COOK'S TIP

Add a little spice to this potato bake dish by incorporating 1 teaspoon of chilli powder at Step 4, if wished.

This simple dish is delicious as a main meal. Choose good sausages flavoured with herbs or with flavourings such as mustard or leek.

Tomato *and* Sausage Pan-fry

1 Cook the sliced potatoes in a saucepan of boiling water for 7 minutes. Drain thoroughly and reserve.

2 Meanwhile, heat the vegetable oil in a large frying pan over a medium heat. Add the sausages and cook for 5 minutes, turning the sausages frequently to ensure that they are browned evenly on all sides.

3 Add the onion pieces to the pan and cook for a further 5 minutes, stirring the mixture frequently.

4 Stir in the tomato purée, red wine and the passata and mix together well. Add the tomato wedges, broccoli florets and chopped basil to the pan-fry and mix together carefully.

5 Add the parboiled potato slices to the pan. Cook the mixture for 10 minutes or until the sausages are completely cooked through. Season to taste with salt and pepper.

6 Garnish the pan-fry with fresh shredded basil and serve hot.

SERVES 4

600 g/1 lb 5 oz potatoes, sliced
1 tbsp vegetable oil
8 flavoured sausages
1 red onion, cut into 8 pieces
1 tbsp tomato purée
150 ml/5 fl oz red wine
150 ml/5 fl oz passata
2 large tomatoes, each cut into 8 pieces
175 g/6 oz broccoli florets, blanched
2 tbsp chopped fresh basil
salt and pepper
shredded fresh basil, to garnish

NUTRITION
Calories *458*; Sugars *11 g*; Protein *21 g*;
Carbohydrate *34 g*; Fat *25 g*; Saturates *8 g*

⭐⭐⭐   moderate

🕐   5 mins

🕐   30 mins

 COOK'S TIP

Omit the passata from this recipe and use canned plum tomatoes or chopped tomatoes for convenience.

Filled with potatoes, cubes of beef and leeks, these pasties make a substantial meal. They are also perfect snacks for a summer picnic or barbecue.

Potato, Beef *and* Leek Pasties

SERVES 4

1 tbsp butter, for greasing
225 g/8 oz waxy potatoes, diced
1 small carrot, diced
225 g/8 oz beef steak, cubed
1 leek, sliced
225 g/8 oz ready-made shortcrust pastry
plain flour, for dusting
15 g/½ oz butter
salt and pepper
1 egg, beaten, for glazing
crisp salad, to serve (optional)

1 Lightly grease a baking tray with butter. Mix the diced potatoes, carrots, beef and sliced leek in a large bowl. Season well with salt and pepper.

2 Divide the pastry equally into 4 portions. Roll out each portion on a lightly floured work surface into a 20-cm/8-inch round.

3 Spoon the potato mixture on to one half of each round, to within 1 cm/½ inch of the edge. Top the potato mixture with the butter, dividing it equally between the rounds. Brush the pastry edge with a little of the beaten egg.

4 Fold the pastry over to encase the filling and crimp the edges together.

5 Transfer the pasties to the prepared baking tray and brush them with the beaten egg to glaze.

6 Cook in a preheated oven, 200°C/400°F/Gas Mark 6, for 20 minutes. Reduce the oven temperature to 160°C/325°F/Gas Mark 3, and cook the pasties for a further 30 minutes.

7 Serve the pasties with a crisp salad, if wished.

NUTRITION
Calories *419*; Sugars *2 g*; Protein *18 g*;
Carbohydrate *38 g*; Fat *23 g*; Saturates *9 g*

 challenging
10–15 mins
50 mins

🖐 COOK'S TIP

Use other types of meat, such as pork or chicken, in the pasties and add chunks of apple at Step 2, if preferred.

This is a variation of an old favourite, where a creamy mashed potato and carrot topping is piled thickly on to a delicious beef pie filling.

Carrot-topped Beef Pie

1 Dry-fry the beef in a large frying pan over a high heat for 3–4 minutes or until sealed. Add the onion and garlic and cook for 5 minutes, stirring.

2 Add the flour and cook for 1 minute. Gradually blend in the beef stock and tomato purée. Stir in the celery, 1 tablespoon of chopped parsley and the Worcestershire sauce. Season to taste with salt and pepper.

3 Bring the mixture to the boil, then reduce the heat and simmer for 20–25 minutes. Spoon the beef mixture into a 1.2-litre/2-pint pie dish.

4 Meanwhile, cook the potatoes and carrots in a saucepan of boiling water for 10 minutes. Drain thoroughly and mash them together.

5 Stir the butter, milk and the remaining parsley into the potato and carrot mixture and season to taste with salt and pepper. Spoon the potato on top of the beef mixture to cover it completely. Alternatively, pipe the potato over the top, using a piping bag.

6 Cook the carrot-topped beef pie in a preheated oven, 190°C/375°F/Gas Mark 5, for 45 minutes or until cooked through. Garnish with a few sprigs of fresh flat-leaved parsley sprigs and serve piping hot.

SERVES 4

450 g/1 lb lean beef mince
1 onion, chopped
1 garlic clove, crushed
1 tbsp plain flour
300 ml/10 fl oz beef stock
2 tbsp tomato purée
1 celery stick, chopped
3 tbsp chopped fresh parsley
1 tbsp Worcestershire sauce
675 g/1 lb 8 oz floury potatoes, diced
2 large carrots, diced
25 g/1 oz butter
3 tbsp skimmed milk
salt and pepper
fresh flat-leaved parsley sprigs, to garnish

NUTRITION
Calories 352; Sugars 6 g; Protein 28 g; Carbohydrate 38 g; Fat 11 g; Saturates 6 g

 moderate

10 mins

 1 hr 15 mins

POTATOES

This is a delicious supper dish for all of the family. Use good-quality herb sausages for a really tasty pie.

Potato, Sausage *and* Onion Pie

SERVES 4

2 large waxy potatoes, unpeeled and sliced
25 g/1 oz butter
4 thick pork and herb sausages
1 leek, sliced
2 garlic cloves, crushed
150 ml/5 fl oz vegetable stock
150 ml/5 fl oz dry cider or apple juice
2 tbsp chopped fresh sage
2 tbsp cornflour
4 tbsp water
75 g/2¾ oz mature Cheddar cheese, grated
salt and pepper

1 Cook the sliced potatoes in a saucepan of boiling water for 10 minutes. Drain thoroughly and reserve.

2 Meanwhile, melt the butter in a frying pan over a medium heat. Add the sausages and cook for 8–10 minutes, turning them frequently so that they brown on all sides. Remove the sausages from the pan and cut them into thick slices.

3 Add the leek, garlic and sausage slices to the pan and cook for 2–3 minutes.

4 Add the vegetable stock, cider or apple juice and sage. Season to taste with salt and pepper.

5 Blend the cornflour with the water until smooth. Stir it into the pan and bring to the boil, stirring until the sauce has thickened. Spoon the mixture into the base of a deep pie dish.

6 Layer the potato slices on top of the sausage mixture to cover it completely. Season with salt and pepper and sprinkle the grated cheese over the top.

7 Cook in a preheated oven, 190°C/375°F/Gas Mark 5, for 25–30 minutes or until the potatoes are cooked and the cheese is golden-brown. Serve hot.

NUTRITION
Calories 399; Sugars 6 g; Protein 14 g; Carbohydrate 39 g; Fat 22 g; Saturates 11 g

 moderate

5–10 mins

40 mins

The sauce for this pie is flavoured with rich dolcelatte cheese and walnuts, which are delicious with broccoli.

Potato *and* Broccoli Pie

1 Cook the potato chunks in a saucepan of boiling water for 5 minutes. Drain thoroughly and reserve.

2 Meanwhile, heat the butter and vegetable oil in a large frying pan over a medium heat. Add the pork and cook for 5 minutes, turning until browned.

3 Add the onion and cook for a further 2 minutes. Stir in the flour and cook for 1 minute, then gradually stir in the vegetable stock and milk. Bring to the boil, stirring constantly.

4 Add the cheese, broccoli, potatoes and walnuts to the pan and simmer for 5 minutes. Season with salt and pepper, then spoon the mixture into a pie dish.

5 Roll out the pastry on a lightly floured work surface until 2.5 cm/1 inch larger than the dish. Cut a 2.5-cm/1-inch wide strip from the pastry. Dampen the edge of the dish and place the pastry strip around it. Brush with milk and put the pastry lid on top.

6 Seal and crimp the edges and make 2 small slits in the centre of the lid. Brush with milk and then cook in a preheated oven, 200°C/400°F/Gas Mark 6, for 25 minutes or until the pastry has risen and is golden. Serve hot.

 COOK'S TIP

Use a mature Cheddar cheese instead of the dolcelatte cheese, if you prefer.

SERVES 4

450 g/1 lb waxy potatoes, cut into chunks
25 g/1 oz butter
1 tbsp vegetable oil
175 g/6 oz lean pork, cubed
1 red onion, cut into 8 pieces
2½ tbsp plain flour
150 ml/5 fl oz vegetable stock
150 ml/5 fl oz milk
75 g/2¾ oz dolcelatte cheese, crumbled
175 g/6 oz broccoli florets
25 g/1 oz walnuts
225 g/8 oz ready-made puff pastry
plain flour, for dusting
milk, for glazing
salt and pepper

NUTRITION

Calories *616*; Sugars *8 g*; Protein *22 g*; Carbohydrate *53 g*; Fat *37 g*; Saturates *10 g*

★★★ moderate

🕐 5–10 mins

🕐 45 mins

This pie contains chunks of pineapple – a classic accompaniment to ham – with potatoes and onion in mustard sauce, and a cheese-flavoured pastry.

Potato *and* Ham Pie

SERVES 4

225 g/8 oz waxy potatoes, cubed
25 g/1 oz butter
8 shallots, halved
225 g/8 oz smoked ham, cubed
2½ tbsp plain flour
300 ml/10 fl oz milk
2 tbsp wholegrain mustard
50 g/1¾ oz pineapple, cubed

pastry
225 g/8 oz plain flour, plus extra for dusting
½ tsp dry mustard
pinch of salt
pinch of cayenne pepper
150 g/5½ oz butter
125 g/4½ oz mature Cheddar cheese, grated
2 egg yolks, plus extra for brushing
4–6 tsp cold water

NUTRITION

Calories *887*; Sugars *10 g*; Protein *31 g*;
Carbohydrate *68 g*; Fat *57 g*; Saturates *34 g*

easy

10 mins

55 mins

1 Cook the potato cubes in a saucepan of boiling water for 10 minutes. Drain thoroughly and reserve.

2 Meanwhile, melt the butter in a saucepan over a low heat. Add the shallots and fry gently for 3–4 minutes until they begin to colour.

3 Add the ham and cook for 2–3 minutes. Stir in the flour and cook for 1 minute. Gradually stir in the milk. Add the mustard and pineapple and bring to the boil, stirring constantly. Season well with salt and pepper and add the potatoes.

4 Sift the flour for the pastry into a bowl with the mustard, salt and cayenne. Add the butter and rub it in until the mixture resembles breadcrumbs. Add the cheese and mix to form a dough with the egg yolks and water.

5 Roll out half of the pastry on a lightly floured work surface and use to line a shallow pie dish.

6 Spoon the filling into the pie dish. Brush the edges of the pastry carefully with water to seal.

7 Roll out the remaining pastry and press it on top of the pie, sealing the edges. Decorate the top with the pastry trimmings. Brush the pie with egg yolk and cook in a preheated oven, 190°C/375°F/Gas Mark 5, for 40–45 minutes or until the pastry is cooked and golden. Serve immediately.

This dish is very filling, and only requires a simple vegetable accompaniment or some bread.

Curried Stir-fried Lamb

1 Cook the diced potatoes in a large saucepan of boiling salted water for 10 minutes. Remove the potatoes from the saucepan with a slotted spoon and drain thoroughly.

2 Meanwhile, place the lamb cubes in a large mixing bowl. Add the curry paste and mix well until the lamb is evenly coated in the paste.

3 Heat the sunflower oil in a large preheated wok over a medium-high heat.

4 Add the onion, diced aubergine, garlic and grated ginger to the wok and stir-fry for about 5 minutes.

5 Add the lamb to the wok and stir-fry for a further 5 minutes.

6 Add the stock and cooked potatoes to the wok, bring to the boil and leave to simmer for 30 minutes or until the lamb is tender and cooked through.

7 Transfer the stir-fry to 4 warmed serving dishes and scatter with chopped fresh coriander. Serve immediately.

SERVES 4

450 g/1 lb potatoes, diced
450 g/1 lb lean lamb, cubed
2 tbsp medium-hot curry paste
3 tbsp sunflower oil
1 onion, sliced
1 aubergine, diced
2 garlic cloves, crushed
1 tbsp grated fresh root ginger
150 ml/5 fl oz lamb or beef stock
salt
2 tbsp chopped fresh coriander, to garnish

NUTRITION
Calories 375; Sugars 6 g; Protein 26 g; Carbohydrate 27 g; Fat 19 g; Saturates 6 g

  easy

10 mins

1 hr

 COOK'S TIP

The wok is an ancient Chinese invention, the name coming from the Cantonese, meaning a cooking vessel.

Bread *and* Cakes

The potato adds an interesting flavour and texture to loaves and cakes. This section includes a range of unusual recipes, and also shows the qualities of the sweet potato in combination with fruit and spices, such as the Fruity Potato Cake, which is ideal for any special occasion. There is also a tempting plaited loaf and some smaller treats, such as the delicately spiced Potato & Nutmeg Scones, which are perfect to serve on any occasion.

This bread has a delicious cheese and garlic flavour and is best eaten straight from the oven, as soon as it is the right temperature.

Cheese *and* Potato Plait

SERVES 8

1 tbsp butter, for greasing
175 g/6 oz floury potatoes, diced
2 sachets easy-blend dried yeast
675 g/1 lb 8 oz white bread flour, plus extra for dusting
450 ml/16 fl oz vegetable stock
2 garlic cloves, crushed
2 tbsp chopped fresh rosemary
125 g/4½ oz Gruyère cheese, grated
1 tbsp vegetable oil
1 tbsp salt

NUTRITION
Calories *387*; Sugars *1 g*; Protein *13 g*;
Carbohydrate *70 g*; Fat *8 g*; Saturates *4 g*

moderate

2 hrs 30 mins

55 mins

1 Lightly grease and flour a baking tray. Cook the potatoes in a saucepan of boiling water for 10 minutes or until softened. Drain and mash.

2 Transfer the mashed potatoes to a large bowl. Stir in the yeast, flour and vegetable stock and mix to form a smooth dough. Add the garlic, rosemary and 75 g/2¾ oz of the cheese and knead the dough for 5 minutes. Make a hollow in the dough, pour in the vegetable oil and knead the dough again.

3 Cover the dough and leave it to rise in a warm place for 1½ hours or until doubled in size.

4 Knead the dough again and divide it equally into 3 portions. Roll each portion into a sausage shape about 35-cm/14-inches long.

5 Press one end of each of the sausage shapes firmly together, then carefully plait the dough, without breaking it, and fold the remaining ends under, sealing them firmly.

6 Place the plait on the prepared baking tray, cover and leave to rise for 30 minutes.

7 Sprinkle the remaining grated cheese over the top of the plait and cook in a preheated oven, 190°C/375°F/Gas Mark 5, for 40 minutes or until the base of the loaf sounds hollow when tapped. Serve while it is warm.

This is a great-tasting loaf, coloured light orange by the sweet potato. Added sweetness from the honey is offset by the tangy orange rind.

Sweet Potato Bread

1 Lightly grease a 675-g/1 lb 8-oz loaf tin with a little butter. Cook the sweet potatoes in a saucepan of boiling water for about 10 minutes or until softened. Drain well and mash thoroughly until smooth.

2 Meanwhile, mix the water, honey, vegetable oil, and orange juice together in a large mixing bowl.

3 Add the mashed sweet potatoes, semolina, three-quarters of the flour, the yeast, ground cinnamon and grated orange rind and mix thoroughly to form a dough. Leave to stand for about 10 minutes.

4 Cut the butter into small pieces and knead it into the dough with the remaining flour. Knead for about 5 minutes until the dough is smooth.

5 Place the dough in the prepared loaf tin. Cover and leave in a warm place to rise for 1 hour or until the dough has doubled in size.

6 Cook the loaf in a preheated oven, 190°C/375°F/Gas Mark 5, for about 45–60 minutes or until the base sounds hollow when tapped. Serve the bread warm, cut into slices.

SERVES 8

1 tbsp butter, for greasing
225 g/8 oz sweet potatoes, peeled and diced
150 ml/5 fl oz tepid water
2 tbsp clear honey
2 tbsp vegetable oil
3 tbsp orange juice
75 g/2¾ oz semolina
225 g/8 oz white bread flour
1 sachet easy-blend dried yeast
1 tsp ground cinnamon
grated rind of 1 orange
70 g/2½ oz butter

NUTRITION
Calories *267*; Sugars *7 g*; Protein *4 g*; Carbohydrate *4 g*; Fat *9 g*; Saturates *4 g*

 moderate

 1 hr 30 mins

1 hr 10 mins

COOK'S TIP

The sweet potato bread makes an excellent base for open sandwiches. Top with thinly sliced cheese, tomato and rocket leaves.

Making these scones with mashed potato gives them a slightly different texture from traditional scones, but they are just as delicious. Serve warm.

Potato *and* Nutmeg Scones

SERVES 8

1 tbsp butter, for greasing
225 g/8 oz floury potatoes, diced
125 g/4½ oz plain flour
1½ tsp baking powder
½ tsp grated nutmeg
50 g/1¾ oz sultanas
1 egg, beaten
3 tbsp double cream
2 tsp soft light brown sugar

1 Grease a baking tray with butter and line with baking paper. Cook the diced potatoes in a saucepan of boiling water for 10 minutes or until softened. Drain well and mash the potatoes.

2 Transfer the mashed potatoes to a large mixing bowl and stir in the flour, baking powder and nutmeg.

3 Stir in the sultanas, egg and cream and beat with a spoon until smooth.

4 Shape the mixture into 8 rounds about 2-cm/¾-inch thick and place on the prepared baking tray.

5 Cook in a preheated oven, 200°C/400°F/Gas Mark 6, for about 15 minutes or until the scones have risen and are cooked and golden. Sprinkle the scones with sugar and serve warm spread with butter, if wished.

NUTRITION
Calories *135*; Sugars *6 g*; Protein *3 g*; Carbohydrate *23 g*; Fat *4 g*; Saturates *2 g*

easy

5 mins

25 mins

 **COOK'S TIP**

For extra convenience, make a batch of scones in advance and freeze them. Thaw thoroughly and warm in a preheated medium–hot oven when ready to serve.

Sweet potatoes mix beautifully with fruit and brown sugar in this unusual cake. Add a few drops of rum or brandy to the recipe, if you like.

Fruity Potato Cake

1 Lightly grease an 18-cm/7-inch square cake tin with butter.

2 Cook the sweet potatoes in boiling water for 10 minutes or until softened. Drain and mash until smooth.

3 Transfer the mashed sweet potatoes to a mixing bowl while still hot and add the butter and sugar, mixing together well to dissolve.

4 Beat in the eggs, skimmed milk, lemon juice and rind, caraway seeds and chopped dried fruit. Add the baking powder and mix well.

5 Pour the mixture into the prepared cake tin.

6 Cook the potato cake in a preheated oven, 160°C/325°F/Gas Mark 3, for 1–1¼ hours or until cooked through.

7 Remove the cake from the tin and transfer to a wire rack to cool. Cut into thick slices and serve with a spoonful of crème fraîche, decorated with a few strips of lemon rind.

SERVES 6

1 tbsp butter, for greasing
675 g/1 lb 8 oz sweet potatoes, peeled and diced
1 tbsp butter, melted
125 g/4½ oz demerara sugar
3 eggs
3 tbsp skimmed milk
1 tbsp lemon juice
grated rind of 1 lemon
1 tsp caraway seeds
125 g/4½ oz dried fruit, such as apple, pear or mango, chopped
2 tsp baking powder

to serve
crème fraîche
few strips of lemon rind

NUTRITION
Calories *275*; Sugars *44 g*; Protein *6 g*; Carbohydrate *55 g*; Fat *5 g*; Saturates *2 g*

 easy

 15 mins

1 hr 30 mins

COOK'S TIP

This cake is ideal for special occasions. It can be made in advance and frozen until required. Wrap the cake in clingfilm and freeze. Thaw at room temperature for 24 hours and warm in a preheated medium-hot oven before serving.

Index